On The Chin

By

Richy Horsley

All rights reserved. The right of Richy Horsley to be identified as author of this work has been asserted in accordance with Copyright, Designs patents Act of 1988.

Printed by
New Breed Publishing
Po box 511
Dagenham
Essex RM9 5DN

info@newbreedbooks.co.uk

Webstite
www.newbreedbooks.co.uk

Copyright Richy Horsley 2002©
Published by
New Breed publishing 2002

First edition June 2002

No part of this book may be reproduced by any means, nor transmitted, nor translated into machine language, without the written permission of the publisher.

A CIP catalogue record for this book is available from the British Library

Printed and bound in Great Britain.

ISBN 0 953855597

Please note: The theoretical information and physical techniques outlined in this book are for self-protection and Self defence purposes only. The author and the publishers cannot accept any responsibility for any proceedings or prosecutions brought or instituted against any person or body as a result of the misuse of any theoretical information or physical techniques described in this book or any loss, injury or damage caused thereby.
All rights reserved.

Dedicated to my father Tom 'Blood' Horsley.

Acknowledgments. Thanks to:

My Mother for helping me with the early years when I couldn't remember that much and without her this book would never have been possible.

Debra Swindells who put some missing links together for me.

Michael Burns who helped me on a few things and for his knowledge on the history of the town and its characters.

Julian Davies for interviewing me for the Streetfighters book and planting the seed for me to write my own book.

Linda for putting up with me for eight years.

Charles Bronson for the excellent tribute.

Gerry Lawson for his wonderful stories over a cup of tea and a bowl of stew.

A special big thank you to my niece Joanne Thomson.

Portrait on front cover by Kelvin Johnson from Shildon, County Durham.

INTRODUCTION

Just before Christmas 1961 Tom and Brenda Horsley had just buried their five month old daughter Alicia and it seemed their world would never be the same again. They couldn't have any more children so they had resigned themselves to the fact that they would be childless. Tom was one of nineteen children but only six reached adulthood and he was the only boy. One of his sisters was called Ruby and she was thirteen years older than him. Ruby was psychic and often gave people readings and was usually spot on. Tom and Brenda lived in a council flat not far from the sea front. One day when Ruby came to visit she said "I can see a pram outside your front door". Tom and Brenda dismissed it as they knew that they couldn't have any more

children together. Over the next twelve to eighteen months Ruby would remind them "I can see a pram outside your front door", "I think a baby is coming from somewhere". Tom and Brenda both knew that this was impossible. Then one day Brenda bumped into an old friend that she had never seen for years. They called her Violet and she was pushing a pram with two little girls in it, one was about ten months and the other was not yet two. Violet said "Haven't you got any kids yet". Brenda replied that she'd had a child and that she'd passed away and couldn't have any more. Violet said that she was carrying again and wished that she wasn't because she didn't want it. Brenda said she wished she could have it and they started talking about adoption. Tom and Brenda went through all the right procedures and in the summer of 1964 Violet gave birth to a baby boy. Six days later Tom and Brenda took home their baby son and called him Richard. Their life was complete again. Ruby's prophecy that she could see a pram outside the front door and a baby was coming from somewhere was spot on.

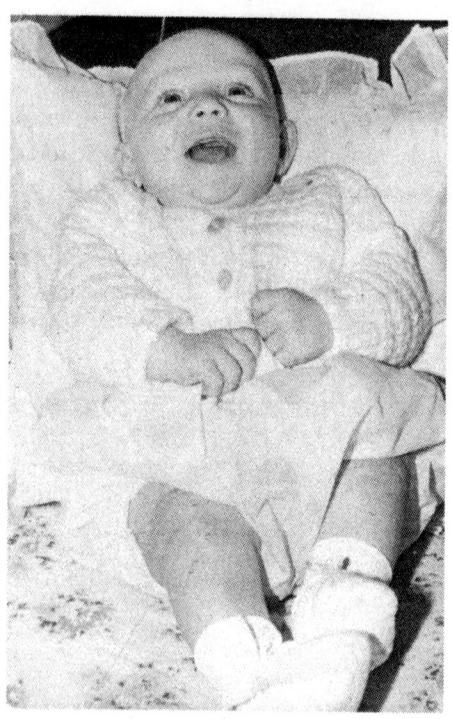

CHAPTER 1

I came from a happy and loving home. I always felt loved and I was never beaten by my parents. My childhood was a happy one. I was told from an early age I was found under a gooseberry bush. When I was five I was told I was adopted, at the time I was gun and holster mad, a bit of a lone ranger. They told me they went to see all these special kids and they picked me out. Waiting for my reaction I looked up and said "Did I have me guns on". Another time around the same age I was out side next door jumping up and down in a muddy puddle absolutely covered. Me mam always had me clean and I always wore shorts. An old lady from down the road walked past and said "Richard, look at the state of you, your mam will go mad. I looked at her and said "fuck off". Me mother found out and took me to her house and I apologised.

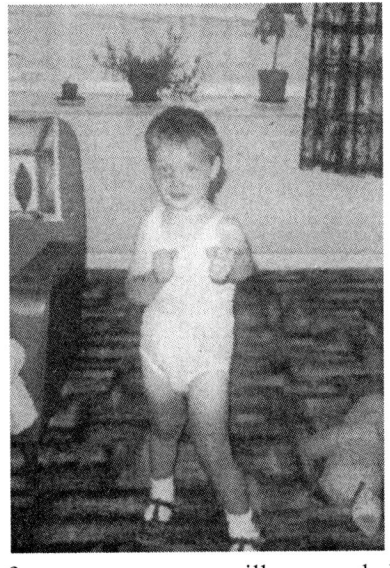

A friend of me mams who was there from day one was called Anne but I called her Bobbin because she used to play a game with me called Roll a Bobbin. That name stuck and to this day she is still called Annie Bobbin and she's now 60. I was horse mad and for xmas Bobbin got me a big spring horse that I could bounce and rock on. I thought I was a real cowboy. In the summer of that year Bobbin took me to Crimdon Dene for the day. We got back at tea time and I wanted to be out with me friends. Me mam thought I'd gone out and closed the door but I was stood on the step and my fingers were still in the door frame, she heard a crunch and me screaming. When she opened the door I was stood their with my finger end hanging off, blood everywhere. I was rushed to the hospital and had it stitched back on. They done a good job but it's still a bit disfigured.

My first memory of getting drunk was when I was five. It was New Years day 1970 and there was a table of drinks in the corner of the room full of bottles, i.e. sherry etc. Me mam and dad went in the kitchen to cook the dinner, me mam asked her friend Bobbin who was with us, to watch me and see that I didn't touch any of the drinks on the table. Bobbin was a bit tired and hung over from the festivities of the night before and fell asleep on the couch. I sat at the table and helped myself to a bottle of QC sherry. I was pissed out of my head and was falling all over the place laughing. Me mother came in the room and said "what's the matter with him", then she spotted the half empty bottle of QC sherry. At that Bobbin woke up and realised what was happening and shouted "I'm sorry, I'm sorry". Me mam said "He will have to go to the hospital" but me dad said "Put him to bed and let him sleep it off" and that's what they did. Me mother was beside herself with worry in case I choked on vomit and was checking on me every ten minutes. When I came back down I was rough and hung over for the rest of the day but one thing that I did do was to eat all my cooked dinner which was a miracle for me as I was a very bad eater. I was practically brought up on Ready Brek and Minodex multi vitamins.

At the time there was a family who lived next door to us called the Weegram's who's son Donald was my age and my friend. One day we were playing a dangerous game seeing how high we could throw darts into the air. Well Donald threw one that came back down and was heading straight for me, I never got out of the way in time and I can still remember that thing hitting me in the back of the neck like a bullet from a gun. I ran in the house screaming in a mixture of shock and pain with the dart still stuck in my neck. I must have looked like the son of William Tell. That was about 1969. Another time me and Donald where in my bedroom while his mam Hilary was having a cuppa down stairs. Normally we were very noisy but this day we were unusually quiet. When Hilary was going they decided to come upstairs to see why we were being so quiet. When they came in the bedroom me and Donald were stood there with knitting needles in our hands and had stripped half the bedroom. Instead of going mad they just laughed their heads off. Not long after the Weegram's moved to the other side of town and I was gutted to have to say goodbye to my pal Donald.

I went into hospital when I was six to have my Tonsils and Adenoids removed. I'd been suffering on and off with them since I was a baby but they wouldn't take me in until I was at least five. So when I started suffering again when I was six they took me in and removed them. The first thing I was given to eat after I'd had them out was a bowl of custard and it killed trying to swallow it. I was in for four days. Nowadays they try to get you in and out within a day because they need the bed space.

The first time me mam and dad heard me swear was in the Easter of 1970. They were looking after my cousin Gary who was a baby in the pram, while his mother went into hospital to have another child. I had just arrived home from infant school with some Easter things I'd been making i.e. cards, baby chicks etc. I went over to his pram to show him what I'd been making and his hands came up and grabbed my things, I shouted in horror "He's got me fucking thing". Me mother still laughs about that one.

About this time I had me first fight. I was always being intimidated by a older and bigger kid who lived around the corner. I would often run in crying after being hit by him. My parents said to me, "Stop running in crying all the time and learn to stick up for yourself". I can remember it was a lovely day and me mam and dad were sat on the step enjoying the sunshine. I went to the corner and seen the bully on the front so I shouted to him and called him a few names, which was like a red rag to a bull. He came after me and I ran to the safety of my parents. When he seen me mam and dad sat on the step he stopped running and started walking towards me, as he got closer something came over me and I started walking towards him. As soon as he was in distance I hit him with as big a punch I could find, it caught him right on the ear and I can remember the pain in his face and tears in his eyes as he walked away. I stood there with my fists clenched ready for more just staring at him, amazed at what I'd just done. I had slain the dragon and he never bullied me again.

I remember a story about a bully that my father once told me. My dad was only young at the time and this bloke thought he could take on the world. He used to pick his fights and loved people cowering in his presence, always growling and intimidating. Now there was a bloke who lived near me dad who was always out exercising, jogging, skipping etc. Everytime that the bully seen him he would call him a big nancy and a fairy and tell him what he could do to him, but the guy just used to laugh and take no notice. One day the bully seen the guy outside skipping and decided it was about time he gave him a good hiding. In those days they used to draw a circle and step inside it and fight, just fists like real men should and you couldn't step outside the circle unless you'd had enough or were carried out. A crowd soon gathered to watch the battlers and the bully got the whipping of his life. He was humiliated in front of everyone and his inflated ego was well and truly burst. It was a lesson to him to stop bullying and to never judge a book by its cover.

CHAPTER 2

There was a family who moved opposite us. The father had just come out of the army and they had been living in married quarters in Germany. His wife and me mam became best of friends. They had a son called Tommy who was my age. The first day I met him he said to me in half English, half German that he was going to stab me. Strange behaviour for a five year old kid I thought. Anyway we became best of friends and even started our first day of school together at Grange primary. Our mothers had dropped us both off and then went to the local shops. Anyway by the time they got home me and Tommy were sat on the step waiting for them as we had done a runner. I see him now and then these days and we are still friends. When I think about it I feel old because we have been friends since the sixties I remember once at me granddads, Sonny 'kid' Morris who was me mam's father and an ex boxer. I was fun fighting in the garden with my cousin 'Tank', he was called Michael but Tank was his nick name. Me dad was in the garden as well and it was a sunny day. Well Tank was older than me and I guess he thought he was just gonna play with me, I got on top of him and he said "Do you want a real fight or a fun fight it doesn't bother me". Whether he said it to make me think "No way, I don't want a real fight with you, your the guv'nor" or whether he had a rush of testosterone I don't know but I was thinking out loud saying "ER", "EM", and looked at me dad and he was laughing and Tank started repeating "I'm not bothered, I will, it doesn't make any difference to me", Then in a split second my mind changed and focused in on the target, the target being his head, and I shouted "Real fight" and let a burst of about ten punches go, left right, left right, all slamming home into Tanks face. Now Tank was a bleeder, he was always having nose bleeds and today was no exception as there was claret everywhere. We both got a telling off and were told to make friends again, when I looked at me dad he was grinning from ear to ear.

A couple of years later Tank had trouble with a friend of mine called Anth and went round to fight him. Now Anth was a boxer and could take care of himself, he was a tough kid and was nobody's fool. When Tank told me he was gonna fight Anth I quietly thought "He is underestimating Anth and is in for a shock". I watched the fight and within seconds Tanks nose was bust, Anth was getting the better of it and Tank changed tactics and took him to the floor, as they were grappling on the deck Tank started scooping up the blood from his nose and was rubbing it in Anth's eyes so he couldn't see, that's when it got split up. Both claimed victory but nobody actually won. Anth was in five national boxing finals as a Junior, he only won one but had some bad decisions against him. Years later he was my corner man at some of my fights.

My first fight at school followed after a fun fight which turned serious and none of us backed out so we started fighting. I remember the lad kept coming at me like a bull, rushing me, but each time he got close I would let a couple of punches go to keep him at a distance because he was stronger than me and if he got me down I probably wouldn't get him off me. He kept coming and I kept hitting, my heart was beating through my chest and my legs were like jelly with the adrenalin because this was for real, when it was broke up by a teacher in the playground there was blood all over me hands and legs off his nose. I was stood outside the head's office in me shorts with me knees shaking uncontrollably. I didn't have it all my own way as I got a black eye and a good ticking off.

Not long after that there was a relation of mine called Tina, her mam was related to my dad and was called Horsley, Tina was my age and went to the same school. There was a lad at school who was picking on her, why lads want to pick on girls I'll never know, she asked me if I would tell him to leave her alone.

I seen her at play time and she showed me who he was. I got hold of him and pointed to her and said "she's my cousin so leave her alone" and then I gave him a taste of his own medicine with a few punches and kicks. He never touched her again.

In late 1970 me mother found out that she had cervical cancer. She went into hospital for a biopsy and was in until Christmas Eve. They wanted her to stay in but she wanted to be home for Christmas so things could be as normal as possible. Three weeks later she went into Newcastle General Hospital and had intense radio therapy treatment and was in there for a full month. I can remember going on the train to see her with me dad and me mam's sister Auntie Ellen. I remember coming out after one visit and me dad was sick in the street. Me mam was then transferred to Hartlepool where she stayed for two more weeks and had a full Hysterectomy operation. After that she had to go for check ups every six weeks for a year, and then it was every six months for two years and then once a year.

When me dad used to go to Newcastle to visit me mam without me, I used to stay at his mam's, me granny Horsley. I remember a cap gun he bought me and a football with Donald Duck and family on it. Donald Duck was my favourite Disney character and I had a big sticker of him on my headboard, you might say I was a bit quackers. Incidentally there was a lad lived near me called Quacker. The wireless used to be on at Gran's so some records I hear will take me back to them times like Marc Bolan's Ride a white swan but the one record that really does is George Harrison's My sweet lord as it was number one at the time and forever being played.

My Step brother John, lived at Gran's. He was a lot older than me and used to take me to the park a lot to feed the ducks and the geese. Gran had a mongrel dog called Kim, which lived to a good old age of about 15 or 16. The three of us used to go for long walks. While I was at Gran's I used to tell Kim to "STAY" while I walked halfway round the block and then I'd shout "HOWAY, KIM, HOWAY" at the top of my voice and run as fast as I could to see if I could get back to Gran's first but Kim always caught me.

Me dad had been married years before he met me mam. He had married someone from West Auckland called Lil and they had three children, Helen, John and Ruth. Lil had also been pregnant with twins when she'd fallen down the stairs and miscarried them. Lil died of T B and Gran brought up Helen, John and Ruth while dad was away working. He was a grafter and roamed all over the country working. He did come home and get a job at the local paper mill so he could be with the kids a lot more. He was a good fighter when he was younger and got the name "BLOOD" Horsley. He was also a friend of the old Streetfighter of yesteryear who was known as "BATTLING" Manners.

CHAPTER 3

When I went into first year junior school, first, second third and fourth years all had dinner at the same time. I got my dinner and sat down and started getting picked on by someone who was in the fourth year. I was scared and didn't dare say anything to him and he spat in my dinner. I keep quiet about it and don't even tell my parents but things like this start the ball rolling when you pretend you are bad or have stomach ache or anything else so you don't have to go to school. The next day it happened again, the same lad picking on me for nothing and the pig spat in me dinner again. It must of made him feel good and made him feel tough that he could pick on someone much younger than himself. Anyway this time I told my parents. There was a lad called Collo in the same year as him and he could have a scrap, my parents knew his so they went round for a word to see if anything could be done. Me dad said to me "At playtime tomorrow go over to Collo and tell him who you are and then show him the lad who's picking on you and spitting in your dinner". Dad said Collo's father will be telling him the story when he gets in tonight so he'll be "expecting to see you tomorrow". The next day at first play I looked for Collo because I couldn't bear the thought of another dinner with spit in it. I spotted him and went over. His name was Michael Collins, Collo was his nick name. I said "I'm Richard and me dad was at your house about someone spitting in my dinner". He said "I know, show me who he is". We looked and then I spotted him and said "There he is". Collo got hold of him and pointed to me and said "Stop picking on him and don't ever spit in his dinner again", then he gave him an unmerciful beating. He knocked seven colours of shit out of him and you should of heard the big brave bully scream. He got a good punching and kicking. I felt bad because I felt like I'd caused it but I hadn't. The bully got what he deserved and never sat near me again in the dinner hall. Me Mam and Dad were glad when I told them what had happened. The problem was nipped in the bud before it got out of hand. If he ever reads this I'd just like to say Thank you, you done me a big favour.

There was a lad who lived near me on the Manor called Tiplady and he was shinning up a drainpipe one day and as he got near the top it came away from the wall and he fell backwards on to the pavement and cracked his head and was left permanently brain damaged. I never attempted to climb a drainpipe after that. Mind you I did get dropped on my head once outside my uncles after my half cousin had me upside down pretending to drop me but kept catching me but this time he missed and BANG I landed on my head. He looked shocked until he seen that I was ok. I remember 1971 when the chopper bike was the craze throughout the nation. It even had gears. The big padded seat was comfortable for your backside and you thought you were one of the blokes from the film Easy Rider on a Harley Davidson. I dreamed of having a chopper. Every time that I saw someone riding one I just used to stare at the bike and wish that I had one. Benny Hill was the Xmas number 1 with Ernie the fastest milkman in the west. On Xmas morning me mam and dad were downstairs shouting look out the window there's Santa. Me dad used to ring this bell and say it was one of Santa's bells off the sleigh. I can hear Santa's bells ringing as I jump out of bed really excited and look out the bedroom window into the dark morning fully expecting to see Santa and co magically flying through the air and maybe even spot me and give me a wave. "I can't see him" I'd say and the bells would stop and I knew he'd have gone to someone else's house but I also knew that he hadn't forgot me so I'd run downstairs and into the room in me pyjamas where the prezzies were. The excitement was unbelievable and me parents used to buzz watching me face. I was playing with me prezzies when my parents said "Come into the kitchen and see what you want for your breakfast". I didn't want to as I was too busy enjoying myself. "You just pick me something" I said but they insisted I had a look. I rushed to the kitchen so I could say "I'll have Ready Break" so I could get straight back to play with my toys but as I went in I was stopped in my tracks and I'll never forget what was in front of me. It was a gleaming brand spanking new chopper bike and it was a blue one. It was the present I'd been dreaming about but never thought I'd actually get. There was a card that said "From Mam, Dad and Santa". I wanted to jump straight on it and go out for a ride but Mam and dad said "Have some breakfast first and then get ready". I couldn't wait to get out on it. A lad called David lived on the end of our block and we used to ride our bikes together and his was bigger than mine but I couldn't wait until he came out and seen me on me chopper and wished he had one. After brekkie I was out on me chopper over the moon with life waiting for David to come out. I was riding up and down wanting people to admire me bike. Then David's door opened and I waited in anticipation for him to come out. He came out first and then his dad followed with David's new bike. When I seen it I nearly fell off mine. I couldn't believe it. It was a brand spanking new gleaming blue chopper, the exact replica of mine, you couldn't tell them apart. He should of got a different colour. David's dad got him some stickers with his name on to put on his bike so there so there was no fighting over whose bike was whose. One day we were arguing and his dad came on the step to see what all the fuss was about. We each had a rope with a not in the end and we were swinging them at each other trying to land first blood. Full blooded swings with each one getting closer to the target. Then the inevitable happened as I landed first and my knot smacked into David's face. He started screaming and his dad took him in and closed the door. I went home victorious. That was the only trouble I ever had with him. On another occasion, Tommy from over the road was getting picked on by David and called names until he reached boiling point. He'd had enough. The lid was about to blow and blow it did. He ran over the road like a madman and laid into David. I think David was in shock as well as pain as Tommy's fists of fury rammed home. Another whipping and another river of tears for David. But he did learn a valuable lesson and that was never to pick on or underestimate anyone because you never know what they are capable of.

CHAPTER 4

When I was about six or seven my dad used to take shots at me with the football outside on the grass. Gordon Banks was the England goalkeeper and I idolised him. I had a big scrapbook dedicated to him. Everytime me dad took a shot at me it was "Save this one Banksie" or "Save that one Banksie". I was playing football all the time against bigger lads who were on their school teams. By the time I was eight I was an established keeper and probably the best in the town for my age. Halfway through first year junior's I changed schools but we still lived at the same address. My parents just thought that the new school had better education. At the new school it was a always a big occasion when the A team played at home, everyone would want to watch and there would always be a good crowd. The strip was light blue with a white hoop around the neck and wrist, light blue shorts and socks. It was a look a like Manchester City strip. The goalkeeper's jersey was solid black and I longed to be wearing it.

In 1972 my idol Gordon Banks was seriously injured in a car accident and lost an eye. He was still England goalkeeper and world number one. I was absolutely gutted. His career was over prematurely. He did make a comeback in America for a time but he said he felt like people were coming to watch a bit of a circus act "Roll up, Roll up, the world's only one eyed goalkeeper". And so he retired from football for good. When he lost an eye I wanted to give him one of mine that's how much I thought of him.

The Mill House Baths and Leisure Centre had just opened in the town. It was always packed out. My Mam and dad used to take me and they'd go in the canteen while I went for a swim. While you were swimming they played all the latest chart music, Nilson's Without You and Donny Osmond's Puppy Love are a couple that I can remember swimming to.

Our Ruth's husband Dave used to take me most of the time to watch Hartlepool United play at home. Him and his mates used to go every week and stand in the same place, they used to get right into it and

give the oppositions players lots of verbal abuse. Their daughter June and me were in the park and we dared each other to jump in the park pond with all our clothes on. We both jumped in and went back to granny Horsley's and said that some lads had pushed us in. The things that you do when your young eh.
I remember watching the young Russian gymnast Olga Korbutt win the gold medal at the 1972 Olympics and a Coca Cola advert with loads of people from different nationalities stood on a mountain top singing "We'd like to buy the world a coke". It was a song by the New Seekers called "I'd like to teach the world to sing" and they released it and it went to number one. Our Helen was known as Nell and she had four kids, Sandra, Graham, Brian and Joanne and I slept at their house quite a bit and we had some great fun.
Also in '72, Me mothers friend Annie Bobbin got married. She was married on my eighth birthday. She had always wanted a child but couldn't have one through medical reasons. She discussed adoption at great length with her husband. Then four years later she finally became a mother when her and Jimmy adopted a beautiful baby girl and called her Joanne.
We used to go round to see my aunt Lois a lot; she married a polish man called Bob Gers. In their back garden they had a pond with big fish in it. They had four children, the oldest was called Janick (pronounced Yanick) and he learned to play the guitar from an early age. Every time we went round our Jan was always playing the guitar. All he did was practice, practice, practice and he kept getting better and better. I remember him playing Rod Stewart's Maggie May in the front room and I realised how good he was getting. He was only young then himself. He joined a band called White Spirit and they were doing gigs in clubs and that. He played in a few bands, with Fish from Marillion and Ian Gillen from Deep Purple. He was such a brilliant player that he had to get a break. Then came the auditions for a guitar player for world famous heavy rock band Iron Maiden. As soon as they heard our Jan play they knew he was the man they wanted. He can make a guitar fuckin' sing. He's now world famous himself and has been on numerous world tours. He wrote the

number one hit single 'Bring Your Daughter to the Slaughter'. He paid his dues and all his hard work paid off. His feet are firmly on the ground. No one deserved it more. A real down to earth great guy and family man. He once told me that he thought the world of my dad, who was his uncle Tommy.

When I went into third year junior's I was playing in goal for the A and B teams. Talk about coincidence, my first game for the A team was at my former school. I was over the moon when I pulled on the black goalkeeper's jersey, it was my time. People were pointing at me and whispering and nodding in my direction when I returned to my Alma Marta. I was still only nine. It was a good baptism for me and we came away with a 2-2 draw. As luck would have it our B teams played each other a few days later and they started moaning saying that I was the A team keeper and shouldn't be playing. We all said the A team goalie was sick so I had stood in for him and they accepted it. Then we stuffed them 3-0.

Our school was protestant and there was a catholic school right next to us called St.Theresa's. In the early seventies both had excellent football teams and were bitter rivals. It was always a big game, the biggest of the season and both always wanted to win so badly. It wasn't just a football match, it was honour and pride as well. I only ever played in one and it was on a Sunday for some reason and it was on St.Theresa's ground. We didn't have a full team because of lads with the flu etc and their coach came over and said " I thought you were supposed to have a good team your school", so we went to the lads houses and begged them to play and we got our squad together. There was a good crowd, everyone gathering in anticipation of a Theresa's win against an under strength Rossmere. Try as they might they couldn't get one past me and at half time we went in 1-0 up. There was only one team in it in the second half as they played us off the field. The pressure was relentless as the crowd were screaming for their team. It looked like a shock 1-0 win was on the cards and it felt like we'd already played an extra ten minutes, plus the ref was their coach. Was he ever gonna blow. Then Theresa's pressure finally paid off when they scored with the last kick of the game to level it at

1-1 and there was a big roar from the crowd. As soon as our player touched the ball to kick off again the ref blew the whistle for full time. They had got out of Jail by the skin of their teeth.

I supported Leeds Utd as a kid up until I was twelve and I've followed Newcastle Utd ever since. Me Mam and dad had friends who lived at the bottom of the street called Harry and Jean and we would often call down to see them. They had 7 kids. I got on well with Tommy who was a year older than me. Tommy is still a good pal now. His dad Harry used to be sitting in his chair and as I walked past he would grab hold of me and knack me. He was a rough old sod. He always made sure he hurt me because he played to rough. He was a big Sunderland fan and at the time I was Leeds mad and they were due to meet in the F.A.Cup final. He would always torment me with "Leeds are crap", "Leeds are rubbish", "Sunderland are the best" and things a lot stronger. Even before the meeting in the final he was a proper nark. Coming up to the final I thought I would go down at full time after Leeds had tortured them and take the mick. Well my nightmare was complete when Sunderland won 1-0. Five minutes later there was a letter delivered to our house addressed to me. When I opened it, it read, SUNDERLAND 1 in very large letters, Leeds 0 in very small letters.

It was sent up by Harry who had the last laugh. I watched every recording of the game hoping that Leeds would score and it was all a bad dream but every time it turned out the same, Leeds had lost.

Me dad was taken ill and had to go into hospital for tests and it was diagnosed as kidney failure. He had to go in for dialysis three times a week for ten hours at a time. At the time we were living in a two bedroomed house on the Owton Manor estate so he continued to go to the hospital for dialysis until they could find us a three bedroomed house so that one of the bedrooms so that one of the bedrooms could be made into a dialysis room. Me mam had to go to the hospital three times a week with him and stay for the full ten hours while they trained her to put him on the dialysis machine. So when we moved into the three bedroomed house it made life easier without me mam and dad having to travel to North Ormesby three times a week which was a very long bus ride in 1973. It took six months before we moved in the new house while they completed the dialysis room. While they were going to North Ormesby, the sister of the ward had a brother who was in Leeds Utd supporters club. He got me some memorabilia signed by Leeds striker Allan Clarke, which was a good talking point with kids at school and football fans.

CHAPTER 5

We moved in the new house which luckily was only about two minutes walk from me granny Horsley's and right near the park. It was at gran's while I was kicking me Donald Duck ball against the wall that I first met Trev, Rob, Kev and Mick. From 71-74 we were the best of pals and done everything together. We were all football mad and I thought that Rob would make it as a pro because he was such a talented player. He played for Rossmere in the 72/73 season when they played the old enemy St.Theresa's in the town cup final on

Hartlepool's football ground, they lost 1-0. We used to go to parks and see who was playing football and challenge them, us against you's, the first one to ten wins. Our challenge was always met and soon their smiles turned serious when we started to play. We never lost a single game.

Football was our lives back then. We did everything that young boys do. We went all over on our bikes, played games like kick the tin, British Bulldogs etc too many to remember. There wasn't just us four playing these games mind you, there were plenty of other kids who lived in the area who all joined in, the more the merrier. These were some of the happiest times of my life. We went through a stage where we used to go in Trev's washhouse and each of us would have a shovel and pretend it was a guitar and Trev also had the upright Hoover which was his microphone and we would sing Slade songs,

C'mon feel the noise and all them. The first record that I ever bought was by Slade called My Friend Stan. Only once was there a bit of trouble and that was when Rob booted me in the face and broke me nose and we had a bit of a scuffle nothing more. We soon sorted it out though, I can't even remember what it was about. I could take a good shot even when I was eight.

I used to be able to do a bit of a Donald Duck impression when I was a kid. I was at a party at Trev's house and done the opal fruits advert in a Donald Duck voice and was rewarded with a mars bar. I do remember a massive pile of dog shit that was all lumpy and looked disgusting that was in Trev's garden and the size of it, must of been done by a great Dane. We overpowered Mick and stuck his hand right in it. It came up to his wrist and everyone ran like hell with Mick in hot pursuit, nearly crying, trying to catch one of us to rub his shitty hand all over us. He never did though and went over home to wash it off as he only lived over the road.

I must have been a born fighter because I was from a loving home and was never beaten or abused, I never turned to it because I was deprived of anything, it was just in me. I never looked for a fight ever, it just used to come my way, follow me around, no matter how much I tried to I couldn't get away from it. By the time I was ten I'd had about fifteen fights, and almost all of them were over after a few punches. But I was always told to expect the unexpected, which has been great advice over the years. I had a fight with a karate bloke's son who thought he was the bees knees, I totally wiped the floor with him and made a mess of him. The karate bloke was supposed to be making an appearance at me uncle's house which was near to where the fight took place, he never turned up so he must of decided to stay at home with a pork chop. I was always a quiet lad so people used to think I wasn't up to much but when they seen me go they sharp changed their minds. Another fight was with a kid people thought was tough because he was loud and the way he went on. They called him Bash and I smashed him to bits, I could of been corny there and say that Bash got bashed but I never. As I was walking home my hands were hurting really bad, I had gotten a bit carried away and punched him on the top of the head a few times. My next door neighbour who was called Mrs.Darley picked me up in her little blue car and dropped me home. She had a lovely big dog called Dillon who loved me. I still have a photo of me and Dillon from when I was about nine. Another fight I had, was arranged when I was about eight or nine. It was outside the baths, I turn around to walk a few meters to get some distance before we begin and I can hear whispering. The next thing I know I was jumped from behind and the lad started to choke me. I was lucky I managed to get him off and I threw him to the floor. I got on top of him and let the punches go smashing into his face and it was all over. Less than fifteen seconds from start to finish. Why hang about in long drawn out fights. You want them to be over as quick as possible and I was blessed with a hard punch. The only drawback is that my hands have been broken so many times over the years. There was a family in the early seventies who lived opposite me granda Morris. One day I was watching out the window my cousin Kevin (Tank's brother)fighting with one of them and was winning when I seen the older brother run out and start knocking hell out of him. I thought I have to do something about this these odds are not fair. I ran out and got tore straight into the oldest brother and gave him a good hiding. Over time I had about four fights with him and chinned him every time and it was always over our Kevin fighting with his brother. Our Kev's dad was my uncle Keith, he was married to me mam's sister Ellen and they had four boys, Michael, Kevin, Steven and Kenneth. He was a coalman and had his own business, he had lads out delivering coal for him and there was always a coal wagon outside their house. He would sometimes come in drunk as a skunk and give all of us kids handful's of money each and we would think we were rich. Sometimes I'd go out collecting with them and I'd be over the moon when people would open the door and I'd say "coal money". We'd be out a couple of hours at night and we'd get fifty pence each which was cushty in them days. It was Keith who knocked me mam and dad out of bed one night. It woke me up as well so I crept on the landing to have a listen because I knew it was something serious. Then I heard Keith tell me mother that her dad had just died of a heart attack. I could hear me mam crying and me dad comforting her as I crept back along the landing and back into bed. Me granda Sonny 'kid' Morris had passed away. He was a amateur boxer way back and a good one and resisted all offers to turn pro. A lad he beat three times became British, Empire and European champion as a professional. He was in the army during the war like most people. Me mam was born in Kettering because that's were he was stationed.

The Horsley's of my family came to Hartlepool almost a 150 years ago. John Horsley was born in 1848 at Wold Newton in Yorkshire. His dad was called Wilson Horsley. John's wife was called Mary Anne Codling and she was from Hinderwell in North Yorkshire and her father was a farmer. They were married in Hartlepool in 1870. In the 1881 census they had five children aged 10,8,6,4 and 2. The youngest being my dad's dad. He was married in 1901 to Mary Allen who was me granny Horsley. Her dad was a true cockney, he was born and bred in Poplar and was a sea sailor. Her mam was from Inverness and was a true scot, She was called MacKintosh. Why they all came to settle in Hartlepool nobody knows. The reason why has gone with them to the grave. Maybe it was just for a fresh start, somewhere new right on the sea coast. But that's how we got here and we are still here. It must be the sea air. My granddaughter Tyler Jo is the fifth generation Horsley on my side to be born in Hartlepool.

CHAPTER 6

Remember the girl called Tina who I stopped getting bullied, her dad was a Scotsman called Jim McKie and a great bloke. It wasn't very often that he was over here as he lived and worked abroad and had done for years. Boxing day '73 he took me and Tank to St.James park to watch Newcastle play Leeds. I was going to see my beloved Leeds, I couldn't wait. After an endless but excited journey (Jim called on a couple of friends) we finally arrived. The crowds of people were unreal, I've never seen this many people in my life. I tried to buy a Leeds rosette but no one had any left. We queued for an hour, slowly getting closer to the entrance. Jim asked his mate to look after us and he'd see us after the match and he went off. Just before we got to the entrance the bloke shouted "No more, the ground is full". I was devastated. We had to think about what to do as Jim had gone. We saw a crowd gathered and you could see in part of the ground and watch the game. I slipped my way through and all of a sudden there they were. My heroes in the flesh, who I'd supported since I could remember and who I'd only seen on telly and in the papers. I was in awe. I took a moment to behold the sight I was seeing amid the pushing and shoving and blokes jostling to get a look and arguing, with the threat that violence could erupt at any moment. Allan Clarke and Supermack weren't playing but everyone else was. I watched Ian Mcfaul the Magpies keeper, he was on the start of match of the day for a while getting a goal scored past him by Alan Clarke. Then I watched Leeds keeper David Harvey, studied him, watched him control his back four like a master. I couldn't take much more of getting banged about so me and Tank got out of the crowd and started walking out into the streets of Newcastle. We just walked and talked and always checked we didn't stray to far from the ground. It got dark early and as full time approached we made our way back. Outside the pubs there was loads of empty Newcastle Brown Ale bottles were people would have been drinking as a lot of the pubs will have been full. We get back to the ground and we look and look. After about 15 minutes we spot Jim and boy is he glad to see us. We were in his care and he lost us for an hour and a half. He was looking for us and panicking because his mate had told him we couldn't get in the ground and went off. It was a great experience for me that day and Leeds won 1-0 with a goal by Paul Madeley. On the way back me and Tank were drinkng out of the same bottle and not wiping the top after drinking and we both got scabby mouths. I've always wiped the bottle ever since.

It was '73 when I was right into Bruce Lee. He'd just burst on the scene with his new style of fighting called Kung Fu. Britain and the world went Bruce Lee and Kung Fu crazy. Anything remotely connected to it was big business. I had Bruce Lee posters all over me bedroom wall and got Kung Fu Monthly without fail. I even done a little bit of kung fu but it wasn't my game and soon chucked it. There was queues outside the pictures everytime a Bruce Lee movie was on. Just before he become world famous he was dead at 32. The world was in shock. Bruce is a legend. Me dad used to nark me and call him Bruce Fruit.

One day a few of us had an idea to make a couple of bob. We all had a bike each and we got two coal sacks each from Keith's coal wagon and went to the beach. The idea was to get two sacks of coal each and sell them for fifty pence a bag and make a quid each. Well we filled the bags up but it was really hard work getting off the beach because the sand was soft. We had to push the bikes because there was no room to sit with two sacks of coal. The key to getting it right was the balance, as soon as it leaned to one side the bags would come straight off. By the time we got to the housing estate where we knew we would sell them, we were wiped out and sweating like pigs. As soon as we shouted "Sea coal fity pence a bag" they were sold straight away. It was a good idea and we made a quid each but we never went again. I wonder why.

At the start of the new season in '74, during a game our coach Mr.Bowsefield came behind my goal and said "I hear you've been calling me names", I paused and thought the only name I call him is his nickname of Bowsie so instead of saying "I'm sure I haven't been calling you names", I said "I only call you" and before I could say

'Bowsie' he cut me off and said "I don't want to know" and walked off. I got dropped from the team. I played a few games for the B team and then I packed in.

On sports day I made a bit of a fool of myself. All the school was out, it was a lovely day as we lined up for the 200 meters. BANG off I shot like a rocket, you'd think we were doing 20 meters not 200. I went a mile in front so to speak but then I was struggling to keep it up as my heart, legs and lungs were on fire. Coming into the home straight my lead was drastically reduced. As a few started to pass me on the run in I collapsed in a heap exhausted and finished last.

We all loved playing rounders. I think I might have been a baseball player if I was a young lad living in the USA. One day we were playing rounders a lad called Paul hit the ball right out the school grounds and started running round for a home run or whatever it's called. To the teacher's and our amazement a dog picked the ball up and ran off with it never to be seen again. Another pal of mine to this day is Tony I'anson, we were in the same class and got our swimming certificates together i.e. 25 yards, 100 yards and quarter of a mile. One day our class was playing cricket and Tony was batting. Well he hit this ball and it looked like a certain six. In a split second I decided to go for a spectacular catch and dived as if I was in goal. Then there was a naughty thud as the corgi ball hit me smack in the eye, instant pain. I had an absolute peach of a shiner that lasted for a while. Years later my pal Tony was in with a crowd and went on an armed robbery with them. When they got there the police were waiting for them, they had been set up by one of their so called pals and Tony got a nice 12 and a half years for his troubles. He kept his head down and done his jail like a man but it should never of happened.

When I was 8 or 9 there was a ginger skinhead lad who chased me a few times for nothing to give me a good hiding. He mustn't of liked my face. Anyway he could never catch me but I was always wary whenever I spotted him. He was about 5 years older than me. Many years later when I was bouncing in a particular pub he came in tanked up with a few of his pals. I was buzzing and hoping that there would be trouble because I'd waited a lot of years to put this ginger bully on his arse. I watched him and his every move like a hawk, if he so much as raised his voice I would be over to destroy the bastard. There was no trouble, so when they left I followed them out of the pub and said a few nasty things to him to see if he would fire up and take the bait but his bottle went and he wasn't having any of it and pissed off. He must of seen the fire in my eyes. I got a little satisfaction out of it even though he never got chinned.

Isn't it funny how songs remind you of particular times. Billy Don't Be A Hero reminds me of primary school. It was a monster hit. There was a couple of great lads from then called Billy Phillips and Michael Leslie. I've never seen any of them from that day to this and wonder what happened to them.

I was still a Leeds fan in '74 but me mates Rob and Kev were Newcastle fans. They were gutted when Liverpool stuffed them in the F.A.Cup final 3-0. The F.A.Cup final was always a big occasion in our house but in 1975 it was a no no for me.

CHAPTER 7

Throughout '74 it was really uneventful and life went on as normal and me dad was doing ok on dialysis. I used to watch me Mam put mud packs on his face and he used to wave at me looking like Al Jolson. One day me auntie Ellen was watching me Mam put me dad on the dialysis machine and was putting these huge needles in his arm, when she fainted and as me Mam turned around she was sliding down the wall a naughty shade of green.

As the New Year turned, me dad started to become ill. He started losing weight and the kidney machine wasn't doing its work. The last ten days of March he became very ill. Me Mam was phoning the hospital to let them know what was happening. They were not able to admit him without a doctor's permission. Me mother had a doctor out every other day hoping they would send him to hospital. The doctors would not send him, they kept telling me Mam to give him different drinks, some of which he was not allowed to have. In the end the hospital he attended sent out a card for a clinic appointment which was the only way to get him to the hospital. When the ambulance arrived they immediately put him on oxygen. The day before he had blacked out a few times but me Mam didn't know it was through lack of oxygen. As soon as they arrived at the hospital he was put on a trolley and wheeled in to see the doctor while me Mam waited in the waiting room. Within minutes a nurse came into the waiting room and told me Mam he'd died. As strange as it may seem, on the morning of his death there was a gathering of grandchildren, nieces and nephews who all came to see him all within minutes of each other, not knowing that he was going into hospital.

The death of my father totally devastated me, he was also my hero, I cried and cried. Me Mam used to play a song at the time called 'For the good times' and if I hear it, it takes me back to that time with a lump in my throat. Another couple of months and I will be going into the senior school but life just wasn't the same and would never be the same again without me dad. I became just a shell of my former self. I remember one morning in class someone said ' Has your dad died', I said 'yes' and did my best not to cry.

I used to be scared of the house because I could feel a presence in there. I didn't know at the time but it was probably just dad saying 'Everything is alright, I'm watching over you'. But I could feel a strong presence in the house and it frightened the life out of me. One time I went round home to get our Jimmy's giro and opened the door and it's on the floor so I picked it up and put it on the little box next to the front door just after I shut the front door so I could pick it up on the way out. My stomach used to turn over with the atmosphere I could feel. I was in and out sharpish so when I get to the front door I go to pick up the giro and it's not there. I wasn't totally dumbfounded by it because I could feel strange goings on were happening. I retraced my steps but I knew I left the giro next to the door on the little box. I knew I did. I know they didn't believe me when I said it had disappeared but what else could I say. Anyway the giro was never cashed. About 18 months later when we moved out of the house the giro was found under the stairs unopened. Explain that one. I went into a shell for a year after me dad died.

The 75 F.A.Cup final between West Ham and Fulham, dad had only been dead 5 weeks and we'd always watched every final together. My cousin Steven came round and watched it with me but it just wasn't the same.

I put a sticker on me Mam's bedroom door and it said 'Alvin Stardust was here, ON AND OFF. When she seen it she said 'You cheeky get'.

We went to Derby before I could say goodbye to my mates at Rossmere. I lived in Stockton Road and the law stated that them on one side of the road went to Brierton and them on the other side (my side) went to Brinkburn. All my mates went to Brierton. There were three people out of the whole school who went to Brinkburn and I happened to be one of them.

We went by train to Derby, there was me and me mam, her brother Phillip, and Aunt Ellen and her four (Tank, Kev, Ste and Kenny).

On the train Philly was playing Elvis songs on a cassette player. We also met a bloke on the train who was in crossroads, he played a character called Carney and he gave us all signed pictures. When we got there Rita said 'Welcome to the house that Jack built and I think she was right. We all had to get bathed in front of the fire in an old tin bath that you see in the old movies. I got friendly with a good looking girl who lived in the next street called Angie. And we all became friendly with a family who's surname was Vighe. We went to the baths and the pictures. We all got new bathrobes from Brentford Nylons, blue ones with a red collar and red on top of the pocket and around the sleeves. They looked just like a teddy boy jacket and we were over the moon with them. I used to practice my Elvis lip in the mirror uh huh. The Bay City Rollers were the big band at the time and Tank even had the Bay City Rollers jumper and the tartan trousers. He looked like a fat Les McKewan. Derby was a welcome break and we made new friends. Me and Angie had a snog before we said goodbye.

We went back about eight months later and had another good time meeting up with old friends. I met back up with Angie and even had to flatten her jealous ex boyfriend. I put the nut into him and a couple of rights and it was the end of him. Tank chased his mate up the street but couldn't catch him. Me mam was thinking about moving there and putting me in a Comprehensive school called Benrose but I wanted to stay in Harlepool. When I started senior school I was still suffering from the death of me dad so I didn't even want to mix with people. I definitely couldn't be bothered with all the 'Who's the best fighter in first year' crap and stayed well away from it all. At the end of first year, a year after my father had passed I started to come out of my shell. I flattened someone from school in the local Burn Valley and I also got caned. The Burn Valley is a recreational public gardens. We had to walk through a part of it when we had swimming or field sports. I had a fight in the park with two brothers. They were staring so I stared back and one of them said 'Who you looking at', I said 'You' so one of them came over to me and as he got close I put a right hand right on his chin and he hit the deck, just at that his brother tried to surprise me but I decked him as well and also put the boot into him for good measure. I was courting a girl called Jill Coser who lived round the corner. I'd had seen her around and about for a couple of years and she went to the same primary school as our Tank. I always thought she was good looking but never thought she'd fancy me. She went to my senior school and used to get off the stop after me. I would stare at her when I got off and she would look at me and smile, i thought she was just being polite but everyday the smiles became bigger and we ended up going out with each other for about 18 months. She was my first love. At Christmas I got her a necklace, it was just something small and it was silver and when you blew it, it would spin round and you'd see the words I love you. I wasn't soppy or nothing, far from it, after all it was Christmas. She bought me the latest single by Queen that I liked called 'Somebody to Love'. Every time I hear that record it always reminds me of her. Tommy who I started school with was round all the time and I was at his a lot as well. There was a canny little crowd of us and we'd go all over together. We used to be at mine quite a lot playing Elvis records or Showaddywaddy or whoever else. It was a bit like a youth club. It took my mind off things. Me Mam stayed at her brothers for a little while so she wasn't on her own to much. When I went round I used to make their kids magic toast and they used to love it. It was only a big dollop of butter in the middle of the bread and put under the grill but they thought it was my secret recipe. Every time I went round they used to ask if I would make them some 'magic' toast.

My uncle Jimmy went to Wembley in '76 to watch Newcastle against Man City in the league cup final. They had a brilliant time even though they lost 2-1. He brought me a few souvenir's back. There was a big Newcastle flag that I put on me bedroom wall, cup final programme and ticket. I've followed Newcastle ever since.

Most of the last round our area supported Man Utd. It gave me great pleasure to laugh like fuck at them and tease them when they got beat by underdogs Southampton 1-0 in the F.A.Cup final in '76.

I ran for the school in the 100 meters hurdles twice. The first race I won. The second race was at Greyfields and all the schools in the town were represented. I wasn't concentrating when the gun went off and they were nearly at the first hurdle before I took off. There were eight in the race and I came sixth. That was the end of my athletics career.

I had a pal called Coto and he had lost his dad a few months before. Now and then he would breakdown and I would do my best to comfort him because I went through the same thing the year before. One night a few of us were talking in the front room when there was a big loud bang on the bedroom ceiling right above us. Everyone ran out of the house screaming and shaken up and wouldn't return. I had to go upstairs and check that everything was ok. There were some weird things going on. In the Feb of '77 we left the house and moved into a caravan for six months. I had a fight when I got home from Derby. I can't remember what it was about now but the lad was older than me and caught me with a couple of good punches. I always fought people who were older than me. My heart and determination and will to win took over as I landed and hurt him and was moving in to finish it when this big fat geezer (he was huge) dragged me away and protected the other lad. As we were arguing because my blood was up and wanted more, victory was mine and only a punch or two away, the dirty cunt sneaked around the fat fucker and hit me with his best shot when I wasn't looking. My lips were bust and came up in no time like inner tubes, I was going mad to get at him but the big fat bastard wouldn't let me and the lad wouldn't fight. He knew my rage would of been taken out on his face. He'd gave me his best shot and it wasn't good enough. So I pissed off and that was that.

CHAPTER 8

I got into the old rock 'n' roll records and for about a year that's all I used to play. My favourite was one by Danny and the Juniors called 'At the Hop.' A year later at the Disco's they would play a couple of rock n roll records and every time 'At The Hop' came on, the dance floor was always full of people rockin and rollin and trying to out dance each other. I even had a teddy boy coat but I only used to wear it in the caravan, my mate Dean ended up with it and he was proper over the moon with it. Ted's had a bit of a mini revival and Happy Days was big on the telly and everyone used to go around thinking they were the Fonz. There was a cafe near the town centre that used to be frequented by all the Ted's and they'd play all the old tunes on the Juke box, Shakin all over etc. There was a cafe in Happy Days run by a big fat guy it was something like AL's or Arthur's I can't remember now but for a while the Ted's tried to get the owners of the cafe to change it's name to the same as the one in Happy Days but they wouldn't. I had a fight at Seaton with a lad called Vic and knocked fuck out of him. One of my aunties was passing and was horrified as she was watching me with hands covered in blood beating fuck out of " Not so tough now" Vic.

Me mother had been seeing a man called Ken for about a year and she said that Ken had asked her to marry him and what did I think about it. Well I had seen that Ken had put a bit of stability and security in her life and she was happy, so as long as she was happy so was I so I said if you want to marry him go ahead and marry him. I made it clear to Ken that he would be my mother's husband but he would never be my father, no one could. I only ever called one man my Dad and would never do it again. As long as I lived no one could ever fill that man's shoes. Ken was happy with that. They got married in May '77 and it was a lovely day and a lot of friends and family turned out. On the photo's I've got shoulder length hair and a white Fred Perry jumper and a pair of blue bell bottoms on. Me mate Tommy is on them and me old girlfriend Jill Coser. I had been going out with her for over a year at the time; I don't really know what

happened between us I think we just drifted apart. You know, like ye do.
After the marriage a few of us went to an old people's home to see me Granny Horsley. It felt like ages since I'd seen her and little did I know but it would be the last time that I ever saw her. She went senile with old age and died a year later.
The news broke that Elvis Presley had just died. They say that he died on the toilet. It would be fitting if he did because it could be said that the king died on the throne. I was a big fan of Elvis and had a good collection of his albums. The media was in a frenzy over it, it was all over the newspapers, television, radio and everyone was talking about it. I loved the king and went into my bedroom to mourn and shed a tear for him. The king is dead, long live the king.
Ken would take us out for day trips and our Kev would come as well and we'd sing Elvis songs in the back of the car, I'm just a Roustabout was a favourite. We wouldn't go too far just other coastal resorts like Morecombe and Whitby. I used to love playing Bar Football and was very good at it. I would always head for the nearest amusements and look for one and if there was I would challenge as many people as possible before we went home. I loved playing Bar Football.
One day in the caravan me mother noticed a square box the shape of a cigarette packet in my pocket and said 'Are those cigarettes in your pocket'. I never answered her and she made me get them out. She said right light one up. She thought she was going to make me sick and that I'd just started smoking but I was a dab hand at it as she soon realised when I smoked it. I started smoking about a year earlier when I used to light her nipper's up from out of the ash tray. She smoked the non tipped ones called Woodbines and sometimes the tobacco would hit you in the back of the throat and burn like hell and taste like shit. She knew she couldn't stop me from smoking but she wouldn't allow me to do it in front of her. Thankfully I gave up the dreaded weed four years ago and will never smoke again. Another time I walked in the kitchen and my nostrils were filled with such a lovely smell my mouth started watering. My mother had been boiling jam and had just took the pan off the boil. I wandered what could

smell so sweet and wanted a taste so I stuck my finger in, JESUS Fucking Christ the boiling jam stuck to my finger and I was in agony and me finger was burnt to hell. I never done anything like that again. When we lived on the caravan site it was three warnings and you were supposed to be off, I don't know how true it was as I got two warnings in the first couple of weeks but I can't think what for. I met new friends when I lived there and it was only a stones throw from the sea front. There was a family of sisters from Norway who all had blonde hair and were a bit tom boyish and I had some good laughs with them. They lived here for a number of years and then they all moved back to Norway. One day one of them pushed me to far and I hit her, as soon as I done it I regretted it. She never fell out with me because she knew it was her fault but I should never of hit her. I seen her in a night club in the early nineties when she was over here on holiday and she said "I've still got crooked teeth where you hit me" and she always laughed about it.

My favourite race horse Red Rum won the Grand National for the third and final time. He ran in the Grand National five times from 73-77, He won it three times and was second twice. I don't think that record will ever be broken.

It was a long bus ride from the caravan site to my school because it was from one end of town to the other. One day during a science lesson there was a few of us larking around with the Bunsen burners and found that if you put the tube over the tap and turned it on then water would fly out of it. Well boys will be boys and we had a dare. The science teacher was bald with a little tuft of hair at the sides so one of us shouted the teacher down about something just trivial. As he started walking back up the classroom one of the lads put the tube over the tap and another turned it on. As the water started to squirt out I picked up the Bunsen burner and directed it towards the science teacher, the water reached him and landed all over his bald head soaking him. I tried unsuccessfully to hide it as he turned round very quick and seen us all in hysterics as we couldn't hold it in as it was just to funny. The teacher stormed down the classroom full of rage and he was looking straight at me and nobody else. He grabbed a hold of me screaming and shouting and wagging his finger in my face when I got him off and pushed him away. He went to get hold of me again and this time I pushed him away hard and told him loud and clear to "FUCK OFF". When I swore at him all the class went " EEEEEEEEEEE" in unison and one of my mates called Terry was giggling with excitement. I stormed out of the classroom with the teacher in hot pursuit. I was wrestling with him as he tried to drag me to the headmasters office and told him to "Fucking get off me". As we got to the stairs I pushed him down them and ran. I ran out of the school and into the Burn Valley. I made sure that I got home at the same time as usual so I didn't arouse suspicion but as I was getting closer the butterflies were getting stronger because as soon as I got in I thought I would hear "What happened at school today" but nothing was said which surprised me. I'm glad we never had a telephone. I stayed away from school for about six weeks because I thought that I would have been expelled anyway but there was no letter from the school and I was left wondering. When I went back my form tutor informed me that the headmaster wanted to see me in his office. I knew exactly what he wanted to see me about and thought that he must want to see me in person and then suspend or expel me. He asked me for my version of the Bunsen burner fiasco so I told him but he kept interrupting me and giving me the version he was told, the true version, and when he said "So then you told Mr. so and so (I'll keep his name anonymous) to Fuck Off". As soon as he said Fuck Off I started laughing because I thought it sounded funny coming from him and he went ape shit. He said he was going to suspend me but decided to give me another chance. It was then that I knew the teacher had kept his mouth shut about being pushed down the stairs because it must of embarrassed him to much to talk about it, I think I would of definitely been suspended then. My pal Corbo was suspended for shouting at a teacher during a cricket match when the teacher was batting, it was teachers against prefects and the school was out watching and the teacher was called Nutall and me pal shouted "Nutall go and Fuck Off and play with your nuts". We thought it was fucking hilarious. If you have ever read the seventies

Skinhead books, well Corbo was the absolute double of the lad on the front cover of Skinhead Escapes. Anyway getting back to my story the headmaster gave me six of the best with the cane (three on each hand) to teach me a lesson so I would think twice about getting in trouble again. My hands were throbbing and on fire, it didn't matter how much you were screaming inside and felt like crying, you never did and you never showed any emotion to the teacher to let him know that you were hurting, you had to be brave and keep it all inside. That was not the end of my punishment however and a few days later in science when I met the science teacher for the first time since the incident I was made an example of so that nobody else would try anything like I did. I was given the cane again, six of the best again, three on each hand and this time it was in front of the whole class, I became a bit of a celebrity so to speak. So that was my punishment and if you think that I got off lightly think again. Just over that incident I got twelve lashes of the cane. If I had the choice I would of had a drop of suspension any day but I never had the choice. One day down the beach I kicked sand in a teachers face while he was sunbathing and I was recognised. Back at school my form tutor said that I had to go and see Mr. so and so and said " You picked the wrong one there Richard". I apologised and got a severe tongue lashing. I had the misfortune of being caned in every year in senior school, first, second, third, fourth and fifth. Just after that I belted a bully in the hall and was nearly caught by a teacher and about the same time I was sort of seeing a lass and her ex boyfriend was saying this and that and I seen him coming from the lockers between lessons. I missed him with the first punch but connected with the second and he folded. Just as I moved away a teacher appeared but had missed who done it and I wasn't pointed out. Another lad, one of the top boys in the year, well there were rumours going around that he'd been saying that he'd do me no problem. I was told of these rumours and I made a mental note of them. One day in the Burn Valley he was coming my way with about six of his pals, his followers more than pals. I walked straight up to him and said "I heard you've been calling me names and want to fight me". I still remember there was snow on the ground and he had a Cromby coat on and a pair of Doctor Martin boots, before he could answer I put the head straight on him BANG. He slipped a bit in the snow and was shook up and dazed so I waited until he steadied himself and then I hit him with a right hand which put him on his arse and in the same movement I volleyed the head off him and it was all over. In two shakes of a dogs tail it was finished. The victory went round the school and how easy I done it and how I was the 'Hardest in the year'.

I got into boxing watching a fighter called Dave 'Boy' Green on sportsnight. I loved his all action non stop style, every fight he had was exciting and he was a crowd pleaser. I think it was '76 when I first saw him on sportsnight and he made an impression on me. I used to listen to all his fights on the radio and then watch the recording on the television. He was my first real boxing idol. He was a country boy from the fens and they called him the Fen Tiger. A true warrior in every sense of the word.

A couple of years later I plucked up the courage to write to him and I got a reply with a signed photo. I was over the moon; I still have the picture in a frame. I lived miles away from the local amateur boxing gyms so if I went it used to take the full night up and at my age I always wanted to be with me mates. I used to go but not often and not as much as I'd of liked to.

Another lad with a big reputation was Buller. He was our Tanks full cousin (their dads were brothers) so you could say he was my half cousin. We had a little trouble over something and he threw a boot at me and it hit me in the head. It was then game on as we squared up I put a left hook straight in to his belly which took the wind out of him and then I put a right on his chin an it was the end of it.

A friend of mine Corbo was having a fight with a lad who I knew would be a bit too much for him. A canny crowd gathered as Corbo was doing ok and was giving as good as he was getting. Then the other lad started scraping me mates face off the wall, as the crowd cringed and me pal was getting his face really messed up, I thought if he wants to play dirty then so can we and I nearly took his head off with a kick from a pair of Dublin boots which ended the fight. Me pals face was a mess from having his face scraped off the wall. If the other lad hadn't resorted to dirty tactics I think he would have won.

I used to see a chunky looking lad who lived on the caravan site walking around with a pair of brogues on. We used to say 'Alright' to each other and that was all. He was a few months older than me and we became really good pals and they called him Jimmy. I watched him have a fight with a 17 year old called Mark who was going in the army. Mark had a brother my age called Mickey and he was always asking people to 'Save me your nipper', he never ever had ciggies of his own but if he ever seen you smoke it was 'Save me some of that' or 'Save me your nipper'. So he got the name Nipper King and it stuck. The fight with Jimmy and Mark was over nipper king. They had a cushty fight on the site and Jimmy done brilliant. The fight finished and one of the Norwegian lasses said "You nearly had him there Jimmy" but I thought Jimmy did have him. I never heard Jimmy give best unless I missed it which was unlikely. I never brought the subject up. Me and Jimmy had some good times together. His mother was broad Scottish and hard to understand. I was with him when the queen came to town on Silver Jubilee day. We were up by the sea front when she came by us waving. He had told his Mam that she got out and spoke to me and him. A little pork pie. I once seen him chin a lass. She was called Gwyneth and her brother was called Rabbi (that was his nickname I can't remember his real name). They lived on the site and were from Wales, I think they eventually moved back there. An argument broke out between Jimmy and Gwyneth. She was a tall bird about six foot two with long ginger hair when all of a sudden Jimmy clagged her right on the button and she went down like a baby giraffe trying to find it's legs. I was shocked that he hit her and can still remember it. When he went to Scotland for a holiday he brought my mother a tartan paper weight back. There was a jiff advert on the telly at the time and it said squeeze a Jiff. Every time it came on Jimmy would say squeeze a miff and laugh his head off. When we moved from the caravan site to down the town Jimmy would always come and see me. A few years later he was riding on a motorbike and hit a patch of oil on the road and skidded and went straight into a lamp post. A couple of days later he died in hospital. I was gutted. I went to his funeral but it took ages for it to sink in. I have some fond memories of Jimmy. Rest in peace my friend.

CHAPTER 9

At age thirteen I got my first court appearance along with four of me mates, Gam, Corbo, Coto and Vaughnie. Someone had suggested going potato picking to earn some extra money. We walked a good few miles to get to the farmers field but there was nobody there, where are all the tatie pickers? Not a tatie picker in sight just a great big haystack. Well, we were only kids and this haystack looked like one of those bouncy castles that you get at the fairgrounds. The guys at the bottom of the haystack were met with bales of hay dropped on their heads. We had great fun wrecking this haystack for about an hour. All of a sudden farmers and farm hands surrounded us, we made a run for it and got caught. Well we got taken to the local police station and after interviews we all got bail (no pun intended) and had to go back the next week to see if we were getting charged. Just our fuckin' luck the farmer was a local magistrate and wouldn't settle out of court. We got charged with criminal damage, when they called out our middle names in court we all laughed like idiots and the judge gave us a roasting. We had to pay six pounds each for compensation and got a conditional discharge for a year.

There was a big lad who knocked about with us called Spike, there was Sammy, Panny, Skinner and many more, too many to mention. We dug an underground camp and when the weather was nice we used to sleep up there. We were surrounded by fields and trees and nature and it made you feel free. I got the flu when I was sleeping there really bad. When you're young you don't want to rest so you end up getting worse. Our camp lasted for about two months before it was demolished.

We all started going to the boxing gym in an old school building. The rat a tat of bags, skipping ropes turning round at blinding speed and the smell of blood and sweat and liniment oil, I don't know how the others used to feel but I used to love it. We all used to get stuck in and it was hard graft. When we used to spar with each other we knew who was tough on the street so we'd try it on and load up and hit each other with our best shots. The lads had a different impression of me after we'd traded punches because there was always blood spilt. We would try to knock each other out. When they landed they bloody hurt. We were never taught how to do this and do that we just used to fight and I had natural ability. If someone had got hold of me then and taught me properly I think I would of gone a long way. After our little wars in the gym we all knew who had what inside of them. We were there three nights a week for about six months.

In the summer of '78 me Mam, ken, me and Corbo went on holiday to Butlins for a week. We had a great time. Me and Corbo were at the disco every day. We met a couple of lads from London, one was called Jeff, I can't remember the other lads name but he was a spurs fan and went to the home games. There was a punk rocker there with a Mohican who was at all the discos and he used to jump about to the boomtown rats and that. One night after the disco he got on the diving board in the outdoor swimming pool and dived in with all his clothes on. Everyone used to think "He's mad him". The last disco you could see all the lasses crying when they were saying their goodbyes to their holiday loves, especially when a slow one came on like Three Times A Lady. We would laugh at them and say 'look at them daft bastards'. Boney M's 'Brown Girl In The Ring' was very big at the time.

When we got back I started going to football practice with a lad from my class called Bob (I'll call him bob to keep him anonymous). He lived above a pub as his parents were publicans. On the days that we weren't at practice he would take shots at me at the back of the pub. I was still knocking about with all the lads as well but this is what 'I' did. I also used to let him punch me in the Jaw for ten pence a punch. He used to absolutely love it he really did. I used to get a pound a day from him and he thought it was worth every penny. In 1978 it was good money. Brinkburn's goalkeeper Jacko got injured and I was asked to stand in for a few games as I'd impressed in training. I didn't want to let anybody down so I said yes. My first game we were at home to top of the league Henry Smith's, I had to be at my best because there was some good players among them. A corner came in with a terrific bend on it and it was going straight in, I leapt at it and was at full stretch and me fingertips deflected it onto the bar, unbelievably it came back of the bar and landed in my hands. It looked like a trick but it was a pure fluke. At that the coach said to Jacko who was watching "You wouldn't of got that one Jacko". We won 4-3. I played a few more games and we never lost any of them and Jacko came back from injury and I packed it in but I enjoyed it while it lasted.

Sometime during the summer I had camped out in our Roy's front garden, on another night I slept on the couch. The house was quiet and in darkness and everyone was in bed. I don't think I was asleep more than an hour when I suddenly woke up. I could feel something behind me but was to frightened to turn around. I tried to ignore it but couldn't. It was like a vibrating current of electricity and the hair on my body was stood on end. It was in the room and I felt it alright. I plucked up the courage to turn around and have a look and when I did, nothing could prepare me for what I saw. I seen an old woman sitting in the chair opposite me and she was raising her head to look at me and I shouted with fear and leapt of the couch like a scolded cat, really terrified. I ran through the kitchen, then into the passage and up the stairs, banging doors with trying to get through them as fast as possible. I barged into Roy and Jean's bedroom white as a fuckin' sheet, I looked like a ghost, now I know where the expression came from when people say 'You look like you've just seen a ghost'. Roy and Jean woke up and wondered what was going on. I told them I had just seen a ghost in the front room and no way was I going back down there. The look on my face should of said it all. Roy went down to check and found nothing but what was he expecting to find, if he'd of walked in the room in total darkness and it was still there I think he would of passed out. He said it was my imagination. I know what I seen and it was a ghost. A real spirit. I slept in the bottom of their son Andrew's bed.

I was a glutton for punishment and I went back to the boxing gym. I asked the lads if they wanted to go back but none of them wanted to so I went alone. There were some good boxers in the gym and I used to spar with them all. I took some pastings but its all part of the learning process. Guys like the Foreman twins Ken and Keith who were both southpaws and smooth operators, I'd watch them work and wish I could box like that. Ken had the best jab I've ever seen. It banged off my nose quite a few times. Big Ronnie was as tough as they come, every time I got out of the ring after sparring with him I'd be banged up with a bust nose or a black eye but I loved it. When he was a younger he was a good Middleweight and he fought the likes of Herol 'Bomber' Graham and other top amateurs of the time. There was Micky who was an excellent Junior and he caught me with a peach of a left hook on the bell at the end of the first and I felt everything drain out of my legs. I had to go another couple of rounds, but that's how you learn to suck it up and fight through it and get experience. There were plenty of good fighters in the gym and you'd see so many so called tough guys come in and get in the ring, take a pasting and suddenly decide that they don't want to be boxers. When lads used to be bust up ,the main trainer ,Duncan, used to say his favourite saying "That's what it's all about" with a smirk. There was Les, Philly, Peter, Lofty, Tommy, Ron K, Big Chris, T.R and many more. There was also a big guy there who used to try to bully you in sparring and he was a southpaw. My first spar with him he was bullying me around the ring so I thought 'fuck this' and when he came back in I hit him with a cracking right hand in the balls. That was the end of that. In the end I could take anything he threw at me and then I'd come back with mine which he didn't like and people would comment on how much I'd 'come on'. Sometime in '78 one of the national newspapers were running weekly stories and profiles of the former Heavyweight champs like Rocky Marciano and Joe Louis. I collected them and read the print off them. I loved Rocky Marciano. For Christmas I got a book called The Encyclopaedia Of Boxing, It had all the world champs in at every weight and the history of the weights. In depth action and brilliant photo's of Marciano, Louis, Ali etc. Also for Xmas I got a 8mm film projector and screen and some fights on film. They were silent and black and white but when the lights went out and the film was rolling it was magical. Marciano-Walcott, Marciano-Louis, Ali-Frazier and plenty more. The lads from school would come round sometimes and I'd put them on. Everyone used to love them. I still have them to this day. I got my medical box and was lined up to fight in the December of '78 but I started to suffer with pains in my legs and heel and had to see the doctor. I was diagnosed as having Osgood-Schlatters disease. I was not allowed to do any physical exercise for a good while. In English it means that I was growing to fast. It's more common in boys than girls and mostly strikes during puberty. It is basically inflammation of the bone where the thigh muscles attach to the lower leg. The symptoms are pain and tenderness just below the knee and there is noticeable swelling. I had to wear bandages around me knees for six months and also had to have me boot heel built up by a quarter of an inch. As soon as there was a bit of wear on them I had to get them re- done. It was a good job flared trousers were in at the time so you couldn't see the bandages on me knees. If drainpipes were in I'd of been well fucked. So the boxing was put on hold for a while.

I was always at the youth club with me pals and once a week used to be disco night, Thursday I think. You'd see lads on the dance floor showing off or trying to act dead cool and pull the birds. Saturday Night Fever and Grease were all the rage and I'll admit I went to see Grease at the local ABC Cinema with a few of me mates. You'd be surprised at how many so called 'hard' lads that would be stood in the queue waiting to see Grease. People would turn up on disco night with 'The Fonz' t-shirts on and other people would be dressed like 'The Fonz'. There were two brothers called the Barnstable twins who used to go to dancing classes, on disco night's the DJ would clear the floor for one record while they and two bewers (females) danced to Greased Lightning. Them two were done up like Danny Zuko and the two bewers were dolled up like Olivia Newton John. They used to think they were fuckin' film stars, a pair of fuckin' prats really. Disco was all the rage and we had some brilliant nights. Sometimes there'd be fighting and sometimes there wouldn't. Big flared trousers, shirts with big fuck off collars (as they got halfway across your shoulders they used to fuck off), Fred Perry jumpers and Dublin Boots or Doctor Martin's. People were always dying their boots different colours. Red was the most popular colour and you'd be forever polishing them with pride until tour face shone in them. Tuxan Red Renovator was the favourite choice. Happy times.

CHAPTER 10

My mate bought the punk rock album 'Never Mind the Bollocks Here's The Sex Pistols' and I would go round and listen to it with him. We used to laugh at the swear words and I ended up getting into it. He dyed his hair and we all laughed and took the piss but he didn't give a fuck. One night at the disco the DJ put on 'Pretty Vacant' and he was up on the dance floor on his own doing the pogo. Everyone used to laugh at him because he was the first one to do it. It was all new to people and it took a bit for everyone to get used to it. Then I dyed my hair and other people did as well and the punk explosion hit and I was on a rollercoaster ride for a year. I started knocking about with a different crowd. A couple of the lads were called Measor and Waller who had both just got out of Detention Centre. I already knew them because they used to go to my school but had left. Everything went punk mad and people followed suit. We'd go to each others houses and listen to any new singles or albums that they had. The Clash, Sham69, X-Ray Spex, Sex Pistols etc, etc. A few of us bought guitars and a mike and would muck about on them in each others houses. Ken borrowed Measor the money to buy a set of drums. He really appreciated Ken doing that for him and paid him back weekly until it was all paid off. We would wear T-Shirts with obscene writing on them, coats and trousers ripped to bits and held together with safety pins and the odd zip. I used to wear a padlock and chain round me neck like Sid Vicious and so did Measor. One night in a one on one fight outside the youth club Measor was getting choked by his padlock and chain before it was broke up by the youth leader. I thought 'Fuck That' and never wore one again after that. The ten o'clock news came on and announced that Sid Vicious had killed himself with a drug overdose while he was on bail for the murder of his girlfriend. I didn't feel anything I just sat there smirking and Ken said 'The Bloody Idiot'. I went to a hairdressers called 'The Knut house' and got a skinhead, it wasn't to the bone it had a bit left on for a reason. Then step two and it was dyed blonde. Then came the finishing touch as I had red question marks dyed into it. I was over the moon with it, it was completely different to what anybody else had and I didn't half get some funny looks from people. I had it like that for about a month. I must of looked like the fuckin' Riddler from Batman but I didn't give a fuck. I wished I got me photo took when had me hair like that so I could show people and have a laugh at it. We were always fighting with people who didn't like punks or couldn't understand us and there was always fists flying in the Burn Valley and at the youth clubs. We started going to a youth club what was full of Bikers who aged from 18-21. They fuckin' hated us. We introduced punk up there. When the DJ put a couple of punk records on for us and we were on the dance floor going off it doing the pogo and that we'd get drinks chucked over us and there'd always be a fight. Usually once a fight started it escalated and everyone got involved. There were some big fuckin' Bikers who used to get in there as well. I started seeing one of the bikers girlfriends on the side as she was to frightened to tell him and wanted it kept quiet. Anyway after a few weeks he found out and wasn't very pleased about it. He and a couple of gorillas came looking for me. It was a Saturday afternoon and I was coming from the town centre when they spotted me. I thought 'This is it then' and made no attempt to run away, instead I walked towards them. I think he was taken back when he seen I wasn't frightened. He wanted to fight me so I said 'Yes'. I was with Measor. As we walked and looked for a place to fight I looked at one of his mates who I knew was a right handy fucker and looked down at his Dublin boots and cheekily said to him 'I suppose I'll be getting a taste of them will I'. He went off it and was gonna set about me but there was too many people on the street. We went to a bit of wasteland which is now a doctor's surgery and health centre. I calmly took my denim jacket off. I done it very slowly, carefully undoing each button as I looked deep into his eyes to let him know that I couldn't give two fucks about him and also to un nerve him if he was having any doubts. The wasteland ran along a busy street and it was Saturday afternoon with people all over but we were getting it on regardless so I handed Measor my coat and we squared up. As he came towards me I snapped his head back with a left jab. I wanted to keep him at arms length and have a look at him and see what he was all about and if he had anything to offer. I kept jolting his head back with left jabs and his eyes were watering. He leapt at me to try to take me to the floor for a wrestling match but I sidestepped out of the way. By now he must of realised his only chance was to get me on the deck and gouge and bite but I was alert to all of this. I never threw one right hand at him. I was sickening him with the jab and softening him up with it and I knew I had him beat. A policeman had been alerted by some frightened old ladies who were walking past and he came running over as the other lads bolted. He was only interested in the fighters. He gave us both a warning and was threatening to lock us up when he asked for our names and addresses. He asked why we were fighting and we said it was over a girl. When he asked me how old I was and I said fourteen he gave me a funny look and wanted my date of birth. Well the biker couldn't believe it and said 'If I knew you were only fourteen I wouldn't have fought you'. When he was asked the same questions he was reluctant to give his age. When he did he said embarrassingly 'Nineteen'. The copper cautioned us both and sent us on our way. One night Me, Measor and Charlie went to this bewers (girl) house and she sneaked us in through the front door and up the stairs into her bedroom. She was with her mate, her mother and father were downstairs so we had to be quiet. Anyway Measor gets in bed with her mate and I've got a grip of the other one while Charlie has to amuse himself. The bed starts to bang as Measor was fucking her mate and there was some moaning coming from her as well. That put paid to my shenanegins as we had to hold the bed to stop it from making so much noise. The inevitable happened as the bedroom door came open and her father walked in. As it opened Charlie hid under the bed and her dad was greeted with us holding the end of the bed and Measor and that lass having sex. Her dad was shouting and punched the wall as Measor dived out of bed with his tail between his legs and we bolted down the stairs and out the house. What a fuckin' performance. Charlie was never found out and sneaked out the house many hours later.

There was a lad who used to hang around with us called Hedge and he had ginger hair and used to spike it up. He was right into the Sex Pistols and used to think he was Johnny Rotten. He stopped wanting to be called Hedge and wanted to be known as Johnny. He hung around for a time and then they moved to Gateshead and I never seen him again. About eight of us went to a punk disco at either Sedgefield or Spennymoor I can't remember which. We were expecting to make friends but all we got was trouble. They would keep barging into us on the dance floor trying to knock us flying and there was a lot of tension in the air. As we left we found out that next week was the big one, the town disco. Eight of us went back through and we got the same treatment. This time we never took any shit and started fighting with them. We were outnumbered like Davy Crocket and the boys at the Alamo. Everybody piled out into the street as we were fighting for our lives totally outnumbered. One of our boys called Tone ran to the van and got a length of thick chain out and wrapped it round a good few heads. The police arrived and stopped the fighting. One of the tyres on the van had been stabbed and there was a bit of damage. The cops told us to change the tyre and Fuck Off immediately or we'd get banged up. We didn't argue with that and done exactly what they said. They mustn't of wanted the paperwork. The song Babylon's Burning by The Ruts reminds me of that night. What a fuckin' adrenalin buzz that was. It was a good talking point for a few weeks. I still had plenty of fights at the biker youthy and like I said before once one of us was at it everyone seemed to join in and it would turn out like a bar room brawl in a cowboy film. This went on for over a year and we had some great times. Punk didn't last to long but it was fuckin' great while it did last. After the scrapes I'd been through I don't know how I'm still in one piece.

There was a garage at the end of our street that sold second hand cars. I used to walk past loads of times a day and there was a baldie geezer with a Doberman dog who used to fiddle there valeting the cars and looking after the place when the boss was out. We would say 'Alright' to each other and then we started to chat. He lived in a bedsit. It was a family who lived in the house and they rented him the front room. He also had access to the kitchen and bathroom. Me, Measor, Waller and a few others used to call round for a chat and a cuppa. We were into all the punk music so when he decided to put his music on we would look at each other with a 'What the fuck is this shit he's playing' look on our faces. We eventually ended up liking it. Al Stewart, The Moody Blues, Supertramp and all stuff like that. We are still friends 23 years later. His girlfriend gave birth to twins three years ago when he was 51 the dirty old bastard. He's had some stick over it. Personally I couldn't be bothered with all that at that age.

I went to a boxing show to watch me mate Les fight the schoolboy champion. It was a terrific scrap and Les won on points. The lad who he beat was Billy Hardy who went on to win the British and European titles as a pro. I wanted to get back home in time for Sportsnight because they were showing a fight from Las Vegas of the American golden boy and new star of boxing. He was unbeaten and was making his first title challenge so I wanted to see what all the fuss was about, his name was Sugar Ray Leonard.

Me and a mate from school called Feather (his surname was Featherstone) went to the pictures to watch the Sex Pistols film The Great Rock 'N' Roll Swindle. We had a laugh at it and I seen a lot of lads there who I hadn't seen for a while. Punk was then on it's last legs, almost dead. For me the film came too late but I still enjoyed it. Me and Feather also went to see the new boxing film by Sylvester Stallone called Rocky 2.

There was a lad who lived next door to me called Roger, he was also in my class. He came to school one day with cuts and bruises after he had a fight outside a youth club with this lad who was a top three fighter at his school. Anyway Roger was on away turf and was winning the battle when the lads mates waded in. That fight alone catapulted Roger into the top flight and everyone was over the moon with him. People looked on him as number two. I was top dog. He was a quiet lad but a big solid lad. He had a dry sense of humour like mine and we had some laughs together. We hardly went to school in the last year we were always nicking off. He used to get money from somewhere but would never tell me where. We would be in the arcades all day or in the shops and cafe's spending money. No one said anything because we looked older than we were. We went in a men's tailors and bought these two trilby hats, they were fuckin beauties. They came to thirty odd quid and Roger settled the bill. If I ever wanted anything he would buy me it. I never asked much because I don't like to take a lend of people. Roger was my mate if he had money or not it made no difference to me. At school one day I said to the lads "I'm sick of this I think I'll fuck off". The lads said I bet you daren't. I just pushed the table away and walked out during a lesson. The teacher was shouting "Horsley were do you think you're going", "Horsley get back here", I just ignored him and kept walking and he never came after me. We also used to go to Roger's house while his Mam was at work and belt the music out. All the latest chart music what we'd bought that day. Echo Beach and all that was in the charts then. Me mother would hear the music coming from next door and thought it was Roger's Mam, not thinking for one minute that it was me and Roger. We always sneaked in the back way down the back street. One day there was a knock at our door, when me Mam opened it there stood the school board man asking where I was. Me mother said that I was at school. The school board man said I hadn't been for two months. When I got home me Mam said "How was it at school today" and I said 'ok' she said "Why was the school board man here today looking for you then", I just started laughing. I was nearly left anyway so it made no difference. I would normally go to school and get my mark and then leave. Roger told me he'd done karate for a few years and was one grade away from being a black belt and packed it in. I encouraged him to go back and said I'd go with him. We did it for a few months but I wasn't to clever with me legs. He was good so I used to challenge him to kung fu fights in the back street, no hands just kicking. We would go at it hurting each other with full blooded kicks and fight for about 30 mins at a time. We would put each other on the deck and you'd always get up and come back harder and we'd always have bust noses and cut lips and grazes. Roger earned my respect with our little kung fu sessions in the back street and we would always shake hands after it as if nothing had happened. We went in a sports shop one day and came out with a pair of trainers each, a couple of T-shirts each and a pair of satin boxing shorts apiece because I said I was thinking about going back to the boxing gym. I got red and white ones because those were the colour Dave 'Boy' Green wore. I would shadow box in the mirror with them on thinking I was the 'Fen Tiger'.

The final exams came and I got three GCSE's. I don't know what subjects they were in or what grades they were because I never went back to find out. In one exam I only wrote my name on the exam sheet and passed the rest of the time with Bruce Lee flick books. Flicking the pages and watching him fighting. When it was time to leave I thought Thank fuck for that. I was never really a school person. They say there the best days of your life; I wouldn't say they were mine. I felt like shouting a line from an Alice Cooper record "Schools out Forever".

CHAPTER 11

I left school at fifteen and my first job was with a local builder who used to do houses up. He wanted a dogsbody who was only young so he didn't have to pay them much. I got the job through the job centre and never liked it. He expected you to know what you were doing straight away. The hours were long. I was only working for him a week and he told me I wasn't what he was looking for. He really thought he would do. He was a fuckin' arrogant wanker and if I was a bit older I'd of chinned him for sure. I'd been toying with the idea of going back to the boxing gym.

I was sat at home one night waiting for something to come on television, I can't remember what, when there was a newsflash and they went live to the scene. The Iranian Embassy siege was taking place and the SAS were getting ready to storm the place. Me, my mother and Ken watched it all unfold live on TV. When the SAS shot the bombs in and there was explosions and smoke everywhere, and stormed in and killed the hijackers and saved the hostages, it was something else. It made me feel proud to be British. SAS men are true hard bastards.

The boxing season had just ended but I decided to go and see if the gym was open. The amateur boxing season runs from the end of September until the end of May. When I got there it was open. The main trainer Duncan White was there and he was pleased to see me. We had a talk and I said I wanted to come back training. There was a lad in the ring shadow boxing, he was a very good prospect who'd been an amateur for years and in another six months he would be a pro. He'd just had a good third round win in Norway. As I warmed up I thought to myself "Have a couple of rounds with him and see if you've got what it takes". I'd sparred with him before but was always a punchbag. I asked him to spar and he said 'sure'. The bell went and I went straight for him, jab, jab, one, two, left hook, right hand, I was really up for it. He was experienced and I think he got a shock when I went for it. He came back at me just as hard and we could of fought in a telephone booth. Neither of us would give an inch as we traded full blooded shots toe to toe, head and body. We were both bloodied and after two rounds Duncan said " That's enough or you'll kill each other". I'd satisfied myself that I did have something inside me and it was a fighting spirit. I decided then that I wanted to give boxing a go. I started doing roadwork (jogging) as well to build up my stamina. It's amazing how much fitter you get by doing roadwork.

I got home one afternoon and me Mam was in bed bad, she had stomach pains. When Ken got home from work he phoned the doctor. The doctor called an ambulance and me Mam was rushed in and had her appendix taken out. She was in for a week and it was the time of the Moscow Olympics and it was always on the TV in the ward with the great races of British rivals Coe and Ovett.

On one visit I had a pair of two tone trousers on that I'd just bought. A lot of lads I hung around with were Mods, it was the second coming of the Mods and there was vespas flying about all over, everyone was wearing parkas with union jacks on, Madness were big, Ska, The Specials, The Selector, Bad Manners. The only mod thing I ever wore was the two tone trousers. I always wore a donkey jacket or an Arrington, jeans and doctor martin boots and had a skinhead. I used to like dancing to bad manners, I was different but I was just being me. We had some great fun at disco's and parties and house parties. There was always someone who couldn't handle their drink and more often than not someone would be spewing their guts up. There was Johnny, Decker, Peo, Piggy, Gaffo, Anth, Pod, Taller, Richie, Tesh, Finn, Micky Peart and loads more.

Some of us went to the pictures to see the Wanderers and we'd drive about in Tesh's motor and sing songs from the soundtrack, like they did in the movie. Someone would sing and the rest would do the backing, I'm getting embarrassed thinking about it. There was a certain whistle in the film that the wanderers used and we copied it. People still use the same whistle today twenty odd yeas later.

I started working on sea defence at Middleton beach. It was five days a week on a government scheme for £23.50 a week; I got £19.50 a week until I was sixteen because me Mam still got £4 a week child allowance for me. It was hard laborious work but it built my strength up. It involved wire cages called gabions which had to be filled up with rocks and bricks and stacked along side each other along the beach. Then another level and another and another, altogether there was about eight or nine levels. The hard part was carrying the rocks and bricks up the beach, I spent my sixteenth birthday doing just that. There was two gaffers called Denny and Bill and they would tell tales about the old days, they used to call me Rocky. They'd say "This will build your strength up for fighting Rocky". After eight hours of that everyone went home to put their feet up but I went to the gym to put myself through some more punishment. I'd do an hour and a half in the gym, shadow box, stretch, skipping, sparring, padwork, medicine ball, sit ups, press ups, I was as fit as a lop in those days. I'd be up at seven and walk to work at the beach. I would walk down into Church Street and then through the docks and everyday I'd walk past the famous old ship The Warrior because it was being restored here. One day I got a croggy off Tony, we were belting along when my foot got stuck in the spokes and we both went flying over the handle bars and landed with a thud in a big heap. It was a painful landing as my teeth came through my lip so I had to cancel a fight. My old school mate Feather was working there as well and told me recently that one night he was riding past me on the way home through the docks when I shouted for him to give me a croggy. He said 'No' and carried on. Then he said I chased after him and caught him and dragged him back by the hood on his coat and slipped him a crippler, a left hook to the body. He said he was doubled up in agony and couldn't get his breath and when he thinks about it he can still feel the pain. I honestly can't remember doing it but Feather wouldn't lie about a thing like that so it will be true but I can't recall it.

There were three coaches at the gym, Duncan, Norman and Ernie. Sometimes an old bloke called Frank Pybus would turn up and I would love listening to his stories about the old time fighters. He was a former boxer and later a referee. He had a vast amount of knowledge and a good memory. I bet he could of wrote a brilliant book of his memoirs but he died a while back and all his stories went to the grave with him which I think is very sad.

There was an army bloke who came to our gym training for about a week. "I box for the army" blah, blah, blah. Genuine people don't brag about it. I watched him spar and he'd go at it hard, trying to be the guv'nor for some reason, trying to prove a point. I got in with him one session and he came at me bang, bang, bang. He didn't pull his punches, he would really let fly with them. I noticed if I jabbed him to the body he would parry it which left his jaw exposed. I backed him into a corner and pretended to jab to the body, in boxing that is called a feint, as I threw the 'feint' his left hand came down to parry (a parry is a block) my jab and in the blink of an eye I threw a piledriver of a right hand which exploded off his jaw and his eyes rolled back as he collapsed knocked out in the corner of the ring. He took a little time to bring round and Norman had a bit of a worried look on his face and gave me a bit of a telling off in private and said he could see what was going to happen before it did.

I reached the quarter-finals of the National (N.A.B.C) Championships. I boxed the finalist from the year before and was winning when we clashed heads in the last round and I got cut. I thought someone had thrown water in the ring but it was blood. The ref took one look and stopped it. The lad went on to win the title. I went to hospital and had six stitches put in my left eyebrow. I still trained but didn't spar because my eyebrow needed time to heal. This was around the time John Lennon was murdered. I'd had enough of working on sea defence and got a transfer to George Street working in the stores. My pal Gaffo was working with me. The supervisor was called Bill and was a canny mush, he played a couple of games in goal for Hartlepool Utd in the fifties. We'd serve people with screws, nails, glue, hacksaw blades, etc. We also had a dart board and a couple of sets of darts. The radio was on constantly and there was a little office room with a fire where we'd drink tea and listen to Bill telling stories. I enjoyed my time there. A joiner who worked there made a photo frame for me as I had a signed photo of Alan Minter. Gaffo got sacked for sniffing glue, he thought he'd try the evo stick out to see what happened and was high as a kite when the supervisor caught him. I used to get boxing magazines delivered to keep up to date with what was going on in the boxing world. I returned to the ring and got my eyebrow tested and it held out in a hard fight with a lad from Newton Aycliffe. I won a unanimous decision and had a beautiful black eye the next day. After a couple more wins I was in the North-East Counties final (Junior ABA's) and was up against the best junior Lt-Heavy in the country and last years champion Gary Crawford who'd won 5 or 6 national titles already. He was very tall at 6ft 3in and a very big puncher and stopped me. He backed me to the ropes and hit me with a right, left, right which all landed flush on my chin and took a bit out of my legs. He put everything into them and each one was a fight ending punch. He gave me a very strange look when I was still stood in front of him, the look said "Why haven't you gone down". He caught me in the throat with a big right and it was stopped. I couldn't swallow for days and my throat was sore for weeks. I found out that I was the only person who boxed him in the Championships that year, everyone else pulled out and wouldn't box him. He turned pro and boxed under the name Crawford Ashley, he won the British and commonwealth titles and won a Lonsdale belt outright and also won the European title. I fought the lad from Newton Aycliffe again and got caught with a peach of a right hand that should of decked me but I grabbed hold of him and walked him around until my head cleared. I dropped him with a right and he got up and took a count and the bell ended the round. He retired in the second with a broken thumb which was caused when he caught me in the first with a beauty. I also fought a tall rangy lad from Darlington who was 6ft 4in. I doubled him up on the ropes with body punches and knocked him out with a right uppercut which nearly lifted him out his boots. There were a lot of new lads in the gym, a few joined our club from other clubs like the Boys Welfare. Big Ned was on the comeback trail, there was Carl, Spike, Philly B, Gene, Duane, Lee and plenty more. Duane would later become a well known streetfighter, feared and respected. We also had a young lad called Andy Tucker who later won the Junior ABA title at middleweight and captained Young England against USA. Me and Philly B used to have some proper brain damaging wars with every punch aiming to be the last, plenty of claret was always guaranteed.

During the summer me and Micky Peart went all over together and had some good laughs. He was loud were I was quiet. We had our heads shaved and wore Ben Sherman shirts with braces, Red or Black Arrington jackets, Jeans and Doctor Martins. We'd go drinking in this rough bar called the Cobble Bar. You had to go down a set of steps because it was in a basement. The regulars would eye us with suspicion. They all smoked dope and all got it from the same dealer who was one of them. He would pull out a big bag with different sized and different prised lumps of dope in full view of everyone but nobody ever said anything. He was a big scarey looking man with a stubble who only had to look at you to frighten the life out of you. People would be in and out of the pub all night buying dope from him. Years later I had a fight with him and done him, it also turned out that he was a police informer. The dirty rat. Me and a few lads had a fight down town with some lads from out of town, I started battling with one of them when I fell over some steps, all I could think was 'get up, get up' before he could take advantage, I did and gave him a beating. Luckily my mates came out on top as well. I loved nights like that when I was young.

Another night Me, Gaffo and Kev went in the kebab shop after a night on the piss and ordered three Donna's but none of us had any money left to pay for them. When they put them on the counter and held their hand out for the money, We grabbed them and ran like fuck. As we were running we heard shouting behind us. It was a geezer from the kebab shop with a big machette in his hand chasing after us, Luckily we got away. Talk about Ali Baba and the three thieves.

CHAPTER 12

Every August around my birthday is a fayre called the Hartlepool show, it's just like a carnival. There's a big beer tent, shows, business stalls, raffles to win cars, Helicopter rides, face painting, candy stalls, burger vans, The Waltzers, The Army always do a display. It's only on for two days, a Saturday and Sunday but it's always packed to the rafters and it's a great family day out. The Carnival comes here every summer as well and that's always packed out. It's here for two weeks. On the last day is the traditional parade which brings out loads of crowds.

I never returned to the gym until the first show was three days away. I turned up on a Monday and Duncan said to me " Will you fight Glenn McCrory on Thursday". McCrory's people had been on the dog and bone (phone) to Duncan the night before and asked if I was available for Thursday and he said he'd let them know. I'd boxed on the same show as Glenn a couple of times in the junior ABA's and one of the lads from the gym thought I had the beating of him but I said 'No'. It was on McCrory's own club show and plus I'd never trained for months. If any matchmakers had any last minute problems they would phone Duncan and he'd always pull them out the shit. Duncan had already entered me in the championships (N.A.B.C) which was only two weeks away. I was in at Lt-Heavy and Carl was in at Lt-welter. Carl was the best gym fighter I ever seen. He was half caste with great boxing ability and silky smooth skills. In the gym he wore white shorts with a black stripe and looked like Muhammad Ali and he had the tools to match. I thought Carl would go on to bigger and better things but he never turned pro. He could hit you three times before you landed a punch. He fought twice that day in the championships and his hands came up like puddings. The second fight was a carbon copy of the first, both fights were wars and he dropped both fighters, both in the last last to win decisions. My head was pounding from shouting for him. The lad I fought went on to become a professional bodybuilder, He made history by winning Mr.Universe five times in a row and he's won various strongman competitions, his name was Eddie Ellwood and our fight was a straight final (North East). We were trading punches and I got caught with a couple of head shots and the ref gave me a standing count. I asked him why he was giving me a standing count as I wasn't hurt and didn't feel as if I'd been hit but he took no notice. We carried on trading, when we got in a clinch he was blowing like a whale and I knew he'd nearly shot his bolt and I was sure I would stop him. I missed with a left hook which would have taken his head off. He rallied off another volley of punches, a couple landed but most were taken on my arms and the ref shouted 'stop boxing' and stopped the fight. I told the ref that not once had I been hurt and was never in any danger so why had he stopped it. He waved me away and gave no explanation. I told Duncan I'd had enough and he said " Don't get disheartened, I'll get you a return on a club show". The day of the return I went through the pre fight nerves. I was thinking ' I hope it's not another premature stoppage', 'I'll win this one, I can beat him'. I got weighed in and waited for him to arrive. When he arrived he said he was bad and wasn't fighting. It was an anti-climax for me. I said I was finished with boxing and packed it in. Me and Eddie became friends. I was out drinking all the time down the town with Mickey Peart and the lads. I had a 'Tool' inside my coat one night and someone must of seen the shape of it stick through my coat think it was a gun or something and phoned the police. It was a truncheon and I got a fine over it for carrying an offensive weapon. The following was in the local paper.

TRUNCHEON YOUTH IS FINED £50

A youth carried a home made truncheon in case of attack but it proved an unwise precaution for it led to him being fined £50 for possessing an offensive weapon when he appeared before Hartlepool magistrates yesterday. Richard Stephen Horsley (17) of Dalton Street, Hartlepool, admitted possessing an offensive weapon in Mulgrave Road, Hartlepool, on November 21, 1981.

Sergeant John Ness, prosecuting, said that at 11:30 pm on Nov.21, police officers acting on a tip off saw a Hillman car with four youths inside parked outside a take away. As they approached, the defendant, who was sitting in the back seat, ducked out of sight. The officers asked them to get out of the car and discovered a black wooden home made truncheon concealed beneath the rear seat. The defendant initially denied the truncheon belonged to him, but later said he carried it for his own protection and would use it if there was trouble. Mr. Michael White, defending, said the truncheon had been made by Horsley's grandfather when Kung Fu first became popular in Britain. It had not been made for a "Sinister Purpose". Horsley could not justify carrying the truncheon and had not been in any danger. There was no risk of him using it aggressively.

I went on a coach to Bradford to watch Hartlepool play, there was a few coaches that that made the journey. When we got in, the bit that was allocated to us had loads of their supporters in and both sets clashed straight away as a massive fight broke out. I seen Anth getting stuck in and that's exactly what I did. There was that many people going at it, it was hard to tell who was who and it took the police all their might to stop it. There was plenty of arrests but I wasn't arrested.

I'd often bump into the boxing lads down town drinking and they'd say 'Howay back to the gym', 'Come back and do what you do best' and all that but I wasn't interested. I was having too much of a good time out on the piss. I'd still watch all the fights on the television and got the boxing mags because it was in my blood. Once you've had a taste of it, it never really goes.

One night when I was out I met a lass called Joanne and took her home. Over the next couple of months I'd met her family. I would sit up with her and her dad Jim and we'd talk until the early hours before I made my way home. Her dad was a bad sleeper and was in constant pain with his back and various other problems. He'd been in hospital on numerous occasions for a variety of operations. He was a really nice bloke and we got on great. I'd get invited round for Sunday dinner and there'd be a load of us round the table. Her mam Pat, dad Jim, brothers Paul and Graham, Joanne and her sister Ursulla and me. They welcomed me with open arms and made me feel a part of their family. There was always a card game going on. The next door neighbours would be in and one of Jim's old workmates called Lenny was always round playing. There was always a good atmosphere and plenty of laughs. On a Sunday night they would go to the local club and Jim would hobble round and I'd go sometimes and always have a good time.

One Saturday afternoon I was in the cobble bar with Mickey P having a few pints when I needed to go to the toilet. As I was on the toilet I could hear a commotion coming from the bar. When I went back in it was all smashed to bits. It only took five minutes and the bar, the optics, the jukebox, the table and chairs and all the glasses were smashed to bits. Hartlepool were playing Sheffield Utd and the Sheffield fans had charged into the boozer and wrecked it. No one got a kicking; they were just intent on smashing the place up and left. That was the Saturday, on the Monday I was at court for an assault that happened four months earlier and got remanded for a week. This is what it said in the local paper in March 1982.

EXCHANGE OF WORDS LED TO ASSAULT BY YOUTH

An exchange of words between two sets of youths quickly developed into a case of assault, Hartlepool magistrates heard yesterday. Richard Stephen Horsley (17) of Dalton Street, Hartlepool, admitted a charge of assault occasioning actual bodily harm when he appeared before the court. The magistrates heard that the offence related to November 26 last year. Horsley and two friends were walking along Grange Road when they passed two youths walking in the opposite direction. Words were exchanged between the two groups which eventually spilled over to violence. Horsley punched one of the youths who was left with a cut lip and bruised face. Mr. Barry Gray, defending, said it was a " most unfortunate and disgusting episode ". He said Horsley thought the youth he assaulted had wanted to fight him. "The words 'come on' were spoken by the unfortunate victim and i do not know whether he wanted a fight, but it was taken that way. This wasn't a mugging or unprovoked attack it was something which came out of words exchanged", said Mr.Gray. The Magistrates remanded Horsley to Low Newton for a week while social enquiry reports were drawn up.

While I was in Low Newton I seen Collo, the lad who stuck up for me when that lad was spitting in me dinner in primary school. It had been a lot of years since I last seen him and he never recognised me so I didn't say anything to him. A lad I knew from the Catcote skins called Bonehead got remanded the same day as me but his was for football hooliganism at the Sheffield game. When people said to me 'were are you from' , as soon as I said Hartlepool they immediately thought I was in for football violence because there had been a lot of fighting at the match and a few got remanded for it. Hartlepool might only be a small town (about ninety thousand) but it had a lot of hard men in it and the football fans have hearts as big as lions. There's an old saying that I like and it's very true and it goes " It's not the size of the dog in the fight, It's the size of the fight in the dog". I was taking tablets for bad blood circulation so the first couple of days they put me on the hospital wing. While I was in my cell I heard talking so I looked out and there was a lad I recognised, there was a couple of screws with him and they went in a room. He used to work at George Street when I was working in the stores there, I've forgot his name. Not long after I finished working there he was on the news and in the papers because he murdered his own grandmother over some money and ended up getting a life sentence. He was only sixteen or seventeen when he killed her. I got moved to a wing and was banged up with a lad from Newcastle called Tony. Me mother and our Sandra came to see me and brought me some cakes and sweets. They came again and brought Joanne with them. As they left Joanne whispered in my ear "I've missed my period". I was laying on my bunk thinking, that's all you have to do in there is think, when it dawned on me that there was a chance I could soon be a father. The court day arrived and I was in the cells at the police station, as usual they were full and they put me in with this big fucker called Jimmy, a proper jack the lad. It was the first time I'd seen him, years later I passed him in the street and said to myself "That's him I was in the cells with". A few years after that he was being clever with me in a nightclub because I knocked one of his mates out a few weeks earlier so I went up to him and he stood there glaring cockily at me. I put the nut on him and set about him with both hands and laid him out. He was a mess and the ambulance came and took him to hospital where he stayed for about a week. As I was taken from the cells I was handcuffed to a lad called Ste who I recognised because he used to call at my uncle Roy's years before. He said he knew my face but didn't know where from so I refreshed his memory and he said " I thought I knew you from somewhere ". I call him Maori because he is the double of a Maori. I was called out and went in the dock handcuffed to a screw. I looked around and seen friendly faces, Me Mam was there and our Sandra, Joanne and her Dad Jim, Gibbo and a few others. The jury went out to reach their verdict. It felt like ages till they came back. I had a brilliant social enquiry report and that swayed it for me. The judge said that before my report was read I was getting six months but because I had such a good report I deserved another chance. I was ordered to do 180 hours of community work. I was relieved.

The Falklands war broke out and we would watch every newscast to see what was happening and hoping we wouldn't have too many casualties and that it would be over quick. We won the war but we also had a lot of women who were widowed and it left a lot of children without fathers.

I had been waiting for ages for the Larry Holmes-Gerry Cooney fight to come off and when it did I listened to it live on the radio in the early hours of the morning, about four o'clock. Holmes won in the thirteenth round. They were still fighting fifteen rounds in championship fights then, a year or so later they would be cut to twelve.

Joanne found out that she was definitely pregnant and I was quite chuffed that I was going to be a dad. I started doing my community work. The office were everyone from the area had to meet was through Middlesbrough. I'd get on at the town centre and used to see Eddie Ellwood on the bus going to work at Head Wrightsons. I'd sit next to him and we'd chat for ten minutes before he got off. Everyone got split into groups with different supervisors and off you'd go working all over the place. One week you'd be chopping trees at Helmsley Forrest, the next week painting windows of a community centre or digging gardens over at Eston, a wide range of things. After about a month I started doing three days a week to get the hours done. Joanne took a babysitting job and I'd go with her most of the time. Ken was brought up old fashioned and was sick of me staying out all night and couldn't understand the way I went on. One night my mate Coto stayed and we left all the lights on all night, It was the straw that broke the camels back. Ken went mad with me and we had a big argument in the kitchen. I ripped my shirt off and threw it down and wanted to fight him. Me Mam jumped in and stopped me because I'd of ripped his head off. He told me to get out of his house so I started shouting " Stick your fuckin' house up your fuckin' arse ", " I'll never set foot in this fuckin' house again" and all that and I left. I went to live with Joanne's parents Pat and Jim. I felt a bit homesick for a couple of weeks but settled in nicely. I slept in the bedroom with Paul and Graham. They had bunk beds and put a camp bed in for me. Paul would take turns with me and sleep in the camp bed and I'd get in the bunk. Joanne and Ursulla were in another bedroom and Pat & Jim in the other. They got a video which was all the rage and joined a video club. We'd watch the latest films at night and it was like being at the pictures. I had some great times there and felt more like a son than a son in law. Paul and Graham were more like brothers. One night me and Paul went up our Roy's to watch a boxing film he had on pirate, it was a great copy and an excellent film. Paul said " That's the best boxing film I've ever seen ". The film was Rocky 3. We went back up a couple of nights later and watched it again. Me and Paul started doing a bit of jogging. I thought I'd go back boxing and went to the pro gym to see if I could do a bit of training there and got the ok. The Feeney brothers trained there. John was the British Bantamweight champ and George was in full training for a tilt at the Lightweight crown. I watched them train, watched them spar, talked about various issues and got to know them, especially George. It was a good place to train and it always had a good atmosphere. It was above a pub called The Bird's Nest which has been knocked down now. I also went back to the amateur gym.

I went out to celebrate my eighteenth birthday with the lads and got really pissed, Dancing on tables and falling off and all that, like you do when your eighteen. I woke up the next morning with a monster hangover and Paul told me that during the night he felt something wet and warm wake him up. When his eyes focused he saw it was me pissing all over him. I then got back in bed and went straight back to sleep. Paul had to dive in the bath and Pat stripped the beds. I can't remember a thing.

I fought a 34 year old bloke and was rusty as hell for two rounds and boxed like shite. I upped the pace in the last round to catch the eye and got a taste of snot in my mouth and felt like spewing because it was his. That spurred me on and I hit him with a few good shots and he went down. He was one punch away from being stopped when the bell rang. I got the decision but I was crap. There was a lad from the same club as him who I'd seen fight and was good. He was in his mid twenties and was strong and fit with a good dig. I was fighting him in a few weeks and knew I had to prepare. I went to the pro gym and sparred with Phil Gibson who helped George Feeney prepare for his epic title win (George stopped Ray Cattouse in the fourteenth round in 1982's fight of the year, one of the best domestic fights ever). I'd known Phil a few years and he could fight for fun. He was out of the Jake LaMotta mould and just as tough and was never stopped as a pro. He was in my face all the time making me fight every second of every round; he never took a backward step and made me work very hard. It was just the preparation I needed. I sparred a few times with him for this fight. At the show we were gloved up and ready to go to the ring and we had a stare down back stage. During the first round the left side of my face started going numb because of how hard he was hitting me. As I sat on the stool at the end of the first my eye suddenly closed and then opened again, it was really weird. A few years later Harry Carpenter described in amazement the same thing happening to Sylvester Mitee whose eye swelled up and went straight back down like a flat tyre in front of his eyes. As soon as he said it I said " That happened to me ". You don't like to mention something like that because people will think you are bullshitting. I'd lost the first round but I done my best to win the second, it was hard, the punches were hard, but I had a big heart and kept going forward and trading with him. I thought whoever won the last won the fight. We both sensed victory and fought to a standstill. About 20 seconds from the end of the fight I put everything into a lead right hand and it landed bang on the chin and he went down like a tree being felled. Amazingly he got up and took the count and the ref waved us to box on, I went forward but had nothing left and he back peddled and the bell went. Everyone was cheering. I won a majority decision. The full show was videoed for the Owton Manor Social club in Hartlepool. I have never been able to get hold of the video but I know two people who have seen it. No one seems to know where it is but someone must have it somewhere. The next morning my left eye was completely swollen shut and jet black.

CHAPTER 13

Joanne's waters broke and she went into labour, the ambulance was called and I went to the hospital with her. I think I was more nervous than she was. About six hours later she gave birth and the midwife said "It's a girl". When I held her in my arms I couldn't believe I was a father. She was beautiful and I was so proud. I'll never forget the feeling of being a father for the first time, it was unbelievable, better than winning the lottery. We called her Jill Louise.

We were already overcrowded but now you couldn't move. The council people came out to assess us and see if we had enough points for a house and luckily we did. Within a few days we were offered one so we picked the keys up and went to have a look. After a good look round we decided to take it. After a few weeks wallpapering, painting, getting carpets laid and so on, we moved in. I was playing the father role very well and was very happy. I changed the babies nappies and sometimes bathed her, I took her out in the pram for walks and all the rest of it.

We lived over the road from my friend George Feeney who was the British Lightweight Champion. I started back at the pro gym, I wasn't boxing anymore I'd just go to train and I enjoyed the crack with all the lads. At eight o'clock every morning I'd walk over to George's house and we'd take a five minute car ride and start roadwork. It was over hills and sand dunes, I'd do four miles and George would do eight. He was training for a fight in Italy against the Lightweight Champion of the World Ray "Boom Boom" Mancini. In Mancini's last fight he knocked out and killed a Korean fighter so he just wanted a ten round non title fight, a 'warm up' so to speak. Well he gave Mancini one hell of a fight and almost put him down in the eighth round with a left hook which badly shook him, if he'd of won the last round he'd of got a draw. The fight went out live in the United States and they couldn't praise George enough. They wanted to give him a shot at the title but first he had to beat the number one contender, the American Howard Davis. Davis won the Olympic Gold in Montreal and was voted the best boxer of the games ahead of

Sugar Ray Leonard. I ran on morning's with him leading up to that fight as well. I got to know George and his family quite well and they were lovely people. Davis wouldn't let George near him and boxed beautifully from long range and won the decision. He came over my house with his Lonsdale belt and took some photos of me with it round my waist. It was a
very nice thing for him to do, he won the belt outright. His last fight was in Germany when he was robbed for the European title. It was a twelve round fight and he came on really strong and decked the champion twice. He had a detached retina and decided to retire while still holding the British title. I went to visit him at the eye infirmary in Sunderland and gave him the biography of Rocky Marciano who was his favourite. I regard him as the best boxer ever to come out of Hartlepool and we've had some good un's over the years.

I got a letter from America from the Heavyweight Champion of the World Larry Holmes and in the envelope was also a photo of him in his boxing gear with the championship belt round his waist and on the photo it said "To Richard, Best Wishes, Larry Holmes, The Champ, Peace". I framed it immediately and it's still framed today, it's something I cherish. In his prime I regard him as the second best Heavyweight of all time, Muhammad Ali a close first.

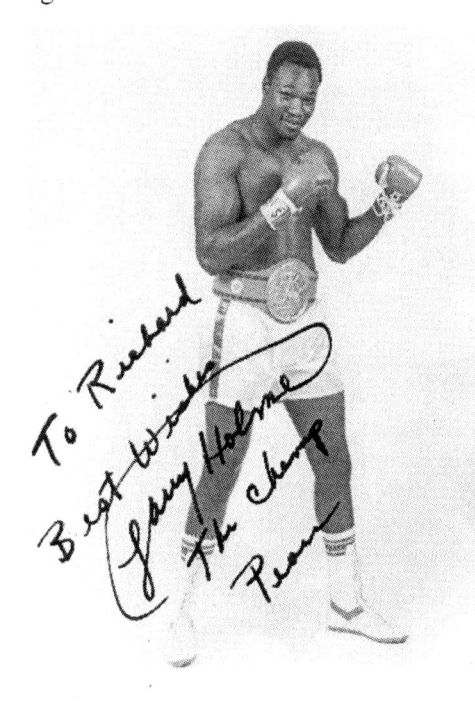

I was corresponding with a bloke from Blackburn called Bob who had the largest collection of boxing magazines this side of the Atlantic. I used to buy old boxing mags called "The Ring" from him. Now and then one would arrive in the post for free with his compliments; he was a really nice man. He sent me a couple of photo's of George Feeney and I got them signed for him and he was well happy. One day years later I was reading the old timers column in the Boxing News and was shocked to learn that he'd died. I was very sad for a few days.

Things at home were starting to get too much for me. Joanne was so moody it was unreal and I was unhappy. She's the most moodiest person I've ever known. I felt suffocated and couldn't take anymore and told her I was leaving. I packed my bags, kissed my daughter and went to live at me Aunt Ellen's. Her second husband Harry got a load of boxing videos from his mate and I would spend hours at a time watching them. Our Kevin and Kenny were still living at home so I shared a bedroom with them. I gave Kenny my red & white satin boxing shorts and he was over the moon, he wore them for ages and wouldn't take them off. I got a job for the council digging gardens over; I stuck it for three month before I got sick of it and packed it in. Ellen was going through some old photo's one day and she passed me one and said "That girl there is your sister". I knew I had two sisters but I'd never met them and didn't know what they looked like and here I was looking at a photo of one of them. The next few weeks' allsorts was going on in my head. I kept looking at the photo and wandered what they were like now? Did they know they had a brother? Did they look like me?

I got home one night after a night drinking and told Ellen that I wanted to meet my sisters but I didn't want to upset my mother. Ellen had a talk to me Mam and she was glad that I wanted to meet them and got in touch with Violet who'd given birth to me. My sisters had always wanted to meet me as well and I was full of butterflies when I went to meet them. Even though we were flesh and blood it was like meeting strangers but we seemed to get on ok. I wanted to grab hold of them and give them both a big cuddle and tell them how much it meant to me by being reunited but I didn't know how they'd react to that so I never said much, I was a bit shy. Debbie was 21 and had given birth to her second child a couple of weeks before. Jackie was twenty and had a little boy. They were both mothers with partners and families of their own, I went to visit each of them on regular occasions but I didn't want them to think I was interfering so I never went to see them as much as I'd liked. I went to Jackie's one night and she was going to visit her mother and asked me if I'd go with her so I said yes. She didn't want to phone her mother to tell her I was coming along, she wanted to surprise her. Anyway we got there and went in the front room. Jackie had this smirk on her face. Her mother whispered to her and nodded in my direction "Who's that" and Jackie said "That's our Richard". After a couple of seconds it sunk in who I was and she let out a yelp and ran out of the room totally embarrassed, Jackie was grinning from ear to ear. Her mother came back in the room and said "Jacqueline, you should have phoned me and I'd of made myself look decent". We had a cuppa and left. Jackie could light up a room with her smile (I say could because she passed away, more of that later) and so can our Debra, both very bonnie girls. I went to the tattooist and got a love heart with two scrolls running through it with Debbie in one and Jackie the other. They didn't have a loving childhood and were often smacked. Their Mam & Dad drank most nights at home and were always fighting with each other. Their Mam would get her hair done every Friday and by Saturday morning you could guarantee it would be rived out. Their Dad Jack was a plumber and worked for the same firm for forty years. One day their Mam just walked out on them and went to live with a bus driver who she'd been seeing on the sly for years. She left a note but no forwarding address. Debbie was in her first year at senior school and Jackie was in her last year of junior school when they arrived home and their mother wasn't there they both had a feeling she had gone. Jack came home from work at dinner time and found the note saying she'd left and went to live with another man. When he got home at tea time he told the kids that she'd gone and wasn't coming back. After that he drank heavily at home every night but still managed to get up for work everyday. They never saw their mother for quite some time as she had moved out of town and got married to the bus driver. In later life Jackie would say to Debbie "Our Richard was the lucky one getting adopted".

I moved out of our Ellen's and got myself a bed-sit. It was owned by a Greek geezer who had a kebab shop. I'd go in now and then to watch for troublemakers but nothing ever happened when i was there. I'd always get anything I wanted to eat and drink for nothing whenever I went in. His son Chrissy came to the tattooist with me and Waller and watched us get back pieces on. Waller got a Pegasus flying through the clouds and never went back to get it finished, he's still only got the outline on to this day as he said it hurt too much. I got Jesus' head with the cross behind it and it takes up the whole of my back, I went back for a few sittings while he done the shading and colouring and I'm glad I did because when it was finished it looked really well.

Johnty D would always be round my bed-sit and we'd have a smoke or go out on the piss or usually both. I was out clubbing all the time, fighting, taking various girls home and having a good time. Joanne used to hover about and one night she said "The baby is bad, I had to get the emergency doctor out tonight", which I knew was bullshit, "You should be with her" and all the rest of it. If the emergency doctor was called then what was she doing out drinking. I think she was just bitter, then she slapped me across the face. I told her not to do it again so she did; she thought she was dead clever. I was telling her to behave or I'd hit her back but she wouldn't take any notice. She slapped me five or six times before I said enough was enough and head butted her and bust her nose, she got the message then.

I was on my way home after a nights drinking one night and was pissed when I tripped and went straight through a shop window. I managed to get up and stagger along the street before the police picked me up and I was charged with criminal damage. At court I was ordered to pay something like six hundred quid compensation, the shop window was big but not that fucking big. I never paid a penny off it and had no fucking intention. Back at court the judge asked why I hadn't paid a single penny off it, I told the truth and said I had no intention of paying anything off it and he gave me three months. I was taken to Low Newton where I stayed for a week. My mate Cliffy was in doing six months and we'd talk about the good nights we'd had. I'd see him going to work in the gardens on a morning and I'd shout a few things at him from my cell window and he'd laugh his head off. Six months later he'd be dead after a fight outside a nightclub.

I was sent to Medomsley Detention centre to do the remainder of my sentence. Detention Centre's were rough horrible places and the regime was just like an army boot camp with physical and mental pressure and everything had to be done at a hundred miles an hour. Most people would pick prison over these places; the idea was along the lines of a short sharp shock. Sometimes it worked, Sometimes it didn't. To be employed there you had to be a pure bastard or you just weren't cut out for the job. They eventually closed all Detention Centres down because they were too brutal. My first day there, the worst screw in the place who was the gym orderly and a right sadistic bastard, marched the new lads off to his office. As soon as you arrived he'd in still fear in you. He screamed at me to "Get a move on" and pushed me hard. I didn't move any faster so he went berserk. First he started slamming me against the wall to knock the wind out of me, then he banged my head off the concrete wall a couple of times and then the punches started raining in on me. I just rode his punches and they had no effect on me at all. I was as cool as a cucumber and I think it unnerved one of the screws a little bit who was watching. The new lads were watching in total shock but other lads who seen it, it was an everyday occurrence to them. I had already made my mark when people seen he couldn't hurt or frighten me, it was fuck all to me. He started screaming in my face and I just answered "Yes sir, No sir". They can make things really hard for you and I wanted to keep my nose clean. About six o'clock every morning the screws would shout "Fall in" and everyone had to run to a certain point to be counted, sometimes people wouldn't hear and would be asleep in bed only to be dragged out of it and kicked. Everyone had to be clean shaven every morning and you only got a couple of minutes to shave. One morning I'd just put the foam on my face when the screw said "Razors in, now". I never got shaved that day but I got away with it where other people wouldn't. During dinner they'd shout out your name if you had any mail. A big ugly screw called Bulldog shouted out my name, he was the screw who watched me stay cool under a barrage of punches on my first day. There was a Boxing magazine for me and he told me he'd give me this one but no more so I had to stop them getting sent in. I never did stop it and they kept sending them in and Bulldog kept giving me them. Good result. The first few days I was there, we were lined up in a corridor and I can hear this growling in my ear. I'm thinking "What the fuck's that"? I turn round and there's this massive lad growling at me. I nearly burst out laughing at him. I look up at him and politely inform him "Who the fuck are you growling at you stupid cunt", "Growl like that again and I'll rip your fuckin' head off do you understand", He nodded yes and stopped. You should of seen the look on his face. Within a couple of days and after a few arguments the word went round that I was the best fighter in the place. I got myself a cushty job in the stores, there was a list of people wanting to work in the stores and I jumped the queue to get it. We were playing hockey one day and the gym orderly said "When you hit the ball don't let me catch anyone raising the stick above knee height", As soon as we started playing that's exactly what one lad did and was promptly laid out. I've seen many lads crying in that place. You had to be quick in the showers because the gym screw would run in shouting "Get out" and belt you round the legs, back, arse, anywhere it landed with a stick. Once a week was the "Fence" which was dreaded. Everyone had to run around the inside perimeter of the fence and there was some very steep inclines which took all the strength out of your legs. It was two miles all the way round but it had to be done twice straight off making it four miles. People would be spewing up, some would cry with pain, the ones at the back got kicked and dragged round. A few hours later we'd be put into teams and have to race each other bunny hopping up and down banks and then piggy back races. It was pure torture and the more pain you were in the more they loved it. If you weren't giving one hundred percent you were punished. When I got out I was glad to see the back of the place. I moved back into the same bed-sit and had a dream I was still in Detention Centre, it was more like a nightmare.

A few weeks after I got out I went to the lakes with Gaffo, Bob, Gibbo and Toddy. We were all pissed and singing "Hartlepool, Hartlepool, Hartlepool", They wouldn't let us in the nightclub and we gave them some frisk. The police came and Gibbo punched one of them and we were all locked up. Gibbo got a hell of a kicking in the cells and was took to court and remanded, I think he got three years at crown court. They let us out after about six hours on the condition that we left town straight away or we'd be locked up, so that's what we did and headed home.

I used to smoke a bit of blow in them days. One night I was drinking round the town and had smoked some blow and went into the nightclub really dizzy. I had words with one of the doormen who was a bodybuilder and he picked me up and threw me through the doors. Everything was in slow motion, almost a dream, as he bounced me off a couple of walls. I couldn't seem to pull myself together and my timing was well out as I missed a few punches. At last I connected with a punch and he went on his arse, I didn't follow up I stood back and just stared at him. He pulled himself together and was mumbling something as he got back up, he brushed himself down and went back in the club. I walked away and realised I was lucky to get away with that one. Another night I was walking past three blokes who were sitting on a pub wall. It was about 11:30 p.m and the biggest one was glaring at me, as I was walking past I said to him "Who are you looking at you fucking doyle". He said "Who the fuck are you calling a doyle" and came at me and swung a big haymaker which I ducked. I had one eye on him and the other on his two mates so I missed with a couple. His mates never moved, they must of been waiting for him to chin me, when I realised they weren't going to jump in I focused in on him because he was trying to take me out and he was a powerful bloke. I moved in distance and landed a big right hand (The Muck spreader) smack on the button and he collapsed in a heap on the deck unconscious. His mates looked at me and never said a word. The big fella was asleep and wasn't moving. I started jogging away from the scene, about every thirty seconds I'd look back to see if he was up but I could see the lads bent over him and he was still stretched out. I had visions of putting the local radio on and the newscaster saying "A man was killed last night in a fight outside a pub" etc. I checked the local papers and there was nothing about it in them and that's when i knew he was ok. I was very relieved.

I was at our Debbie's one night, our Jackie was there as well and Maori Ste called in with his brother H. Maori and our Jackie had been close friends for a few years. H dropped me off at home, years later I would become the best of friends with them both. Another time I was with my mate John and he said it was his sister's birthday and he'd like to go to the club and buy her a drink. I ended up taking her home, her name was Gail, and not long after we ended up getting a flat together on the sea front at Seaton Carew.

At night I'd smoke a little blow and listen to Bob Marley or watch a bit of T.V. When we got to know the couple who lived in the flat below, they said they thought that a family of Rasta's had moved in when they heard Reggae being played all the time. I never went out drinking as much but one night I was with my friend Kevin H in this nightclub and he said he thought there was going to be trouble with the bouncers, it was a quiet night and there was only five of them. I said "Howay then, after you" as it was his fight. We flattened the five of them. Kev's brother was top boy in the town at the time so maybe that's why there was no repercussions.

I went to the pro gym one Sunday morning, I was going past so I popped in to have a look and see who was in. There was a Lt-Heavy going through his paces; he looked very good and as sharp as a razor. He was there to spar but the other man failed to show. Like an idiot I said "I'll spar with you". I'd never had the gloves on for about two years. I took my jacket off and got in the ring in my shoes and jeans, no headguard, no gum shield, just a lion heart. I was knackered after a minute and this lad was as fit as a fiddle and was trying to knock me out with every punch he threw. I soaked up a lot of punishment for nine minutes, (three, three minute rounds), I soaked it up like a sponge but it done me good.

My friend Cliffy was killed in a fight outside the nightclub. He was in the wrong place at the wrong time. There was an argument inside and someone got punched. The person who got punched made a phone call and a van full turned up with weapons and a massive fight broke out. Cliffy was hit with a blow from a baseball bat by accident and staggered over the road and died in the gutter. It was tragic. The lad who got the blame was a friend of mine and a friend of Cliffy's and had known him years. There was no way that it was him but when it went to court about a year later he got life. It was shocking. After a couple of years he was released after an appeal and rightly so. What happened to Cliffy was a tragic accident.

I started doing some jogging on the beach every morning. I'd jog for about thirty minutes, filling my lungs with all that fresh sea air. After a month I felt brilliant but we got a council house and moved to another part of town. Gail was pregnant and we didn't want to bring a baby up in a dingy flat. The house was too far away from our friends and family and we were never happy there, though we got on well with our neighbours Colin and Kathy.

I went to Milton Keynes with some mates to see U2 in concert. There was me, Mickey B, Bone and Chaz. On the way there the car conked out and wouldn't start again as the battery was goosed. At that time an army convoy was approaching with the Colonel at the head in an open top Jeep. They pulled over and the convoy came to a halt. His name was Colonel Collins and he asked what the problem was, we told him it was a flat battery and he got us a jump start and then waved goodbye and the convoy continued on it's travels. We went to the nearest garage and bought a battery and the baby was as sweet as a nut. Not long down the road we came to the convoy, as we flew past we were tooting the horn and saluted the Colonel and he saluted us back with a big smile. At the concert there were thousands of people and we had a brilliant time, U2 were outstanding. My favourite one by them is The Unforgettable Fire and that night they were Unforgettable. We arrived home in the wee early hours wiped out but with some good memories. I still have my concert ticket somewhere.

Me mother bought me an all in one stereo system for my birthday. The turntable on top, then the graphic equaliser, then the radio, then a double tape and at the bottom was the storage space for your records and tapes. I certainly got my use out of that present and was well happy with it.

Gail went to look at a house not far from her mother's because she heard that the couple were looking for a swap. She wanted it and they came to ours to look around and they wanted to swap as soon as possible. Anyway when I went for a look at the house I couldn't believe it, what a coincidence. It was the same house I'd lived in a couple of years earlier with Joanne. I told Gail this but she wasn't bothered and we started preparations for the move.

People know me not only as a fighter but also as a tidy guy and I always treat people with respect. Around this time I got charged with theft. I am not a thief and have never stolen anything in my life. I borrowed a friends video card and got some films out and for some reason they never got returned. The shop called the police and I got pulled in. They had just installed a video camera and of course, I was on it. Now as luck would have it, the day we were moving house was the day I was at court. It's called sod's law and to make matters worse, Gail was nine months pregnant and due anytime. I wanted to be in and out of court as fast as I could so I could help with the house move so I pleaded guilty to get it over and done with. I was waiting for a fine and the judge remanded me for ten days. I was gob smacked. Speechless. Sex cases are always getting bail the dirty filthy bastards and I get remanded for overdue videos. What the fuck's it all about? Because I pleaded guilty I was convicted and got no privileges like other remand prisoners. I wasn't put on the remand wing either but put straight on A-wing. I was in Durham Jail. The next cell to me was a pal from Hartlepool called Sean who was doing eighteen months for assault. I was stuck in that cell for twenty three hours a day and only got out for a walk round the exercise yard with the other cons for one hour a day. The day after I was remanded Gail gave birth to a baby girl, my Mam phoned the prison and they said they'd tell me but they never did. I found out on the eighth day when I got a letter from Gail telling me she'd had a baby girl and called her Donna. After the shock came the emotion and I had a little weep. I wept with joy because I had another daughter and with sorrow because I wasn't there to see her come into this world. The next two days went like two weeks. Finally I was back at court and had a different judge, he shook his head and couldn't understand why I'd been remanded over something so minor. I was ordered to pay three hundred pounds compensation and was released. I went straight to the new house but there was nobody there. I walked there with a lad called Divvy Dave who came to see me at court. I knew she must of been at her Mam's so I went round there. There were a few people there and they all said "Welcome Home". My mother was there and very happy to see me. Gail handed me a little bundle and said "Here's your Daughter". I got a shock when I seen how small she was because I expected her to be bigger. I was a bit scared in case I squeezed her too hard because she was so delicate. I quickly got into changing her nappies and taking her for walks and she was daddies little girl. We used to call her "Shitty". She used to think her name was "Shitty" until she started school because that's all she got called. Take that in the kitchen shitty. Get your coat shitty, etc. I still saw my other daughter Jill on a regular basis. There was a block of flats near our house and my friends Mark and Tracey lived there. They never had any children and there'd always be people in there playing darts and listening to music. You'd be guaranteed a game of darts anytime of the day or night and I had some good nights there.

CHAPTER 14

I made another comeback, this time with the Boys Welfare. I was there for about ten months. It was five nights a week and a Sunday morning and the training was very hard. Before training there was a run, everyone would set off together and you had to be inside a certain time or you were sent out again. Peter the coach would have everything set out so everybody was busy. You'd skip for a round then shadow box for a round, then press ups, pads, sit ups, punch bag, step ups, sprints from wall to wall etc, after each round you'd move to the next exercise which was all numbered so everyone knew what they were doing, we were like links in a chain that was going round. One punch bag exercise was a killer, you had to hit it with two jabs and then a ten punch combination, no more than two seconds to get your breath back and the same again for a full round and then on to the next exercise. After hitting the bag like that you were fucked but it was first class conditioning. Two nights a week after training we'd have to finish off with a little circuit. I don't think I've ever been so fit, I was thirteen stone and rock solid and didn't have an ounce of fat on me. We all got sponsored to do a ten mile run to raise a bit of money for gloves and punch bags and that for the club. One Saturday morning we all met and the coach got his watch out and we all started together. I think my time was about one hour and fifteen minutes. We were like a big family but we trained hard and we sparred hard. You'd think everyone hated each other if you watched a sparring session because it was always heavy. Every time I got in they would always try out there punching power and try to put the big guy on his arse, Welters, Middles, Lt-Heavy but nobody ever decked me, it did keep me on my toes though. There were some really good fighters in the gym and some won national titles. There was Biff, Kev M, Chrissy, Kev C, Graham, Ray, Stewey, Tony, Alan, Garry and others whose names I've forgot. Once I got caught with an elbow and my eyebrow spurted open, Peter said I'd better go to the hospital so they could have a look because it looked like it needed a few stitches. It was the same eyebrow that I got six stitches in years before but this was a fresh cut at the side. They put four stitches straight in it, but this was all part of the game. If you got cut you got cut, so what. Boxing in Hartlepool started on the beach at Seaton Carew where the fighters fought Bare Knuckle. In the early 1900's there was a boxing booth on the corner of Burbank Street known as the 'Blood tub'. It always drew the crowds and you were guaranteed a good punch up. Hartlepool was a booming ship port and someone would go round the Docks and pick five coloured seamen for an 'All In', one in each corner and one in the middle and when the bell rang it was everyman for himself and the winner was the one left standing after some furious toe to toe exchanges. That was always a big crowd puller. During the depression people fought each other for boxes of groceries and if you were lucky you might get a few shillings for fighting six rounds. When Jack Johnson was World Heavyweight Champ back in the early 1900's, Hartlepool had a brilliant boxer called Jasper Carter. People today will never have heard of him but almost 100 years ago he put Hartlepool on the fistic map. In his career he was Lightweight Champion of the North of England for six years, He won the 10st Championship of Scotland and the Middleweight Championship of Ireland. He had 300 fights and most of them were fought over 20 rounds. In his prime he was matched with the then World Featherweight Champion 'Peerless' Jim Driscol. The day before the fight Driscol pulled out and it was the biggest disappointment in Carter's career. Carter fought in front of 80,000 spectators at Celtic Park in Belfast against Irish Middleweight Champion Jack Lavery. Lavery was a stone heavier but Carter produced the goods with a first round knockout stunning the massive crowd. In 1910 he was introduced from the ring with the former World Heavyweight Champ James J. Jeffries and at sometime appeared in a boxing booth in Durham with the legendary Jem Mace. Carter was that confident he could beat anyone in Britain who was his weight he challenged any man to meet him for £100 a side. One night after he'd long retired from the ring, He was in the local cinema watching a film called 'The Set Up' which was about boxing. During the film he became ill and was taken to hospital where he died five hours later aged 63. They don't make them like Jasper Carter anymore, what a fighter.

I done a six mile charity run with my mate Bob. Everyone in the country was doing the run, it was called "Everybody Wants to Run the World" and the pop group 'Tears for Fears' released the record and the proceeds went to charity. Well Id done my bit.

I was working for the council on a job called Site Clearance. There wasn't really that much to do but sit in the cabin and play cards while the supervisor waited for a phone call, we'd only get two or three calls a week, it was an easy job. A lad called Jimmy who I'd done some of my community work with was working with me, also a lad with one arm called Davey who lived around the corner from me was there as well. He got called Davey one arm. Friday was pay day so at dinner time we'd go to the bank and get our wages, have a bite to eat and go to a pub called The Grange and sink a few beers. After a few drinks you didn't feel like going back to work so you either went back late or not at all. The gaffa was cushty and never used to say nowt as long as you never took this piss. There was a three day pop festival held in the town called Dock Rock, it had bands like 'Madness', 'Doctor and the Medics' and all that on. I worked there on security but the festival was a flop and they never held another one.

Gail told me that a lad called Bernie had been trying to tap her up and it wasn't the first time he'd tried. When she said "I'll tell Richy", he said "Tell him, Richy's fuckall". I knew him and were he drank. One night I went to the nightclub with Mark to see if Bernie was in. Mark went in to have a look and came back out and said he was in there with a couple of lads and lasses. I watched and waited from over the road. When they came out I walked over to him and hit him with a right hand that put him straight on the deck, his girlfriend started screaming when I kicked him in the face. He was finished. So much for me being fuckall. My foot was killing and swelled straight up because I only had a pair of soft leather moccasins on; I walked like hopalong Cassidy for about five days.

I tried to get in the Royal Marines. I passed the exam and when I went for the interview I was told I would be a 'risk' and wasn't accepted. Cheeky bastard, I don't know what he meant by a 'risk' because he wouldn't tell me.

Davey one arm came round to mine a few times with some wine what he used to make, it used to blow your head off. One morning at about four o'clock Gail went into labour and as we were waiting for an ambulance Davey one arm was walking past drunk. He came in and said "If it's a boy will you please call it David after me". I told him I'd think about it. As she was giving birth there was a panic because the cord was wrapped round the baby's neck so the forceps had to be used. It was a boy and I was over the moon, every man would like a son. When he came out it took a bit for him to cry. I think we nearly lost him by the look on the nurse's faces but he started to cry and there was a sigh of relief all round. He had two black eyes and marks on his head off the forceps but as each day went by he began to thrive. The nurse said "what are you going to call him". I'd never even given it a thought as I thought it would be another girl but as I opened my mouth I said "Terrance" and that's what we called him.

After I got refused by the Marines I went in the T.A for a few months and went on a two day training course at Ripon. There was about thirty of us from the North-East and we were assessed individually on a wide range of things like the assault course, Drill, Shooting Range etc. On the assault course they wouldn't let you use the rope bridge; you had to dive straight in the water. I don't think I've ever been in water so cold. As soon as you hit it, it took your breath away (it was in the autumn). After two days I came overall fifth which surprised me. I didn't stay very long before I thought "This isn't for me", I'm glad I never got in the Marines.

We moved house and went to the Rossmere area of town. We were near Rossmere park and I'd take the kids there and have a stroll round and we'd feed the ducks. Terry was still a bit too young to understand but Donna used to love it.

My step brother John died aged 40 and left a daughter called Claire who I've never seen since. I was at his house a few months earlier, I never knew then but that would be the last time I saw him alive.

When I was born I was the fourth and final child that Violet bore. Debra was born in 1962, Jacqueline in '63 and me in '64. Violet had also given birth to a baby boy three years before Debra was born and he was adopted. All four of us were to the same parents but the two boys were adopted and they kept the two girls. I seen a thing on T.V were they wanted people to search for lost relatives but you had to make your plea in front of the television cameras. I applied to go on and was accepted so I told Debbie & Jackie and they were excited at the prospect of finding our older brother. I had to go to London for filming and went down by train accompanied by Gail. There was a canny few people there to film their pleas. It was at a big hotel and it was very plush and the T.V Company paid our travelling expenses. The film crew were very nice and it took a couple of takes but I got it right and they were pleased with me. After filming we got reimbursed our travelling expenses and got a taxi to Madame Tussauds, the world famous waxworks museum. It was brilliant and you'd think the dummies were going to come alive because they looked that real, I bet it would be spooky in there at night. We had a good look round before making the long journey back home. The programme was 'Surprise Surprise' hosted by Cilla Black and I was sent two tickets by the T.V company to go back down and see the show but I never went, I watched it at home. Debbie & Jackie were watching as well. During the show Cilla handed over to a bloke called Gordon Burns who was introducing a new thing called 'Searchline' were viewers recorded their own pleas to find relatives and loved ones. He was telling people about the all new searchline and how it worked and then he said "We start with Richard Horsley from Hartlepool" and I came on. I can't remember exactly what I said now but I did have it on tape years ago but it was taped over by accident. I was the very first person ever to be on searchline. We never ever found our brother, he might not have been told he was adopted, we'll never know. I would get pulled up for months after the programme by people saying "I seen you on surprise surprise" or "Did you find your brother". My name wasn't officially changed by deed poll to Horsley until 1979. The name on my birth certificate is Stephen Swindells.

I was doing a bit of security work with a lad called Stewie and he told me about a Doris Stokes book he'd been reading. It intrigued me and I wanted to read it myself so I got it out of the library. I was fascinated by it and wanted to know more about the paranormal. I got the phone number of a well known spiritualist and phoned her up. They called her Ruby and she held meetings every Thursday night so I went along. The meeting were talks, it was all philosophy and she had some wonderful stories of her own, it was all very interesting and what she said all made sense and her meetings were always full. I would just sit there in the background and listen. I'd been going for about four months and the philosophy was excellent but that wasn't enough for me, I wanted more. I wanted proof and I needed my own proof. I decided to stay away for a couple of weeks. I got a photo of my Dad and I was talking to him in my mind every day and told him if he didn't come through and give me some proof I was finished with it and it was all a load of bullshit. I was at Ruby's and the meeting was nearly over and I was thinking "This is my last time but it was nice while it lasted" when all of a sudden Ruby said "I've got a man here called Tom", "Someone here knows him", and she was describing the kidney dialysis machine and all the tubes and how he died and other things about him which were all true and I was sat there speechless and couldn't open my mouth. Then she said

"Someone here has got a photo of this man and they talk to it with their mind". Well that blew me away and that was my proof because I knew it was my father responding to my question. I never said anything but I did write Ruby a letter and told her that message was for me.
Stewie got another job and I was working with a lad called John. He was a good lad with a wife and family and he loved his kids. I asked him one day if he messed about behind his missus back and he said "No way". His kids meant too much to him. He said there was no way he'd lose them over a daft shag what you'd regret for the rest of your life. On one job he'd had, he took beef paste sandwiches to work for his bate for a whole year. It wasn't because he liked them; it was because he gave his family his all. He was a good bloke. About a year later I was shocked to hear that they had split up and it was his wife who was messing about behind his back. He lost his family after all which I thought was very sad and I couldn't help but feel sorry for him knowing it must of broke his heart.
My sister Jackie had post natal depression when she had Stacey so I looked after the baby for a few weeks until she was a bit better. It was the only time she got it.
I started having a knock about with the football again and my mate Robbie would take shots at me. We started going to Brinkburn sports centre once a week for a game of five-a-side which sharpens you up. I started playing in goal for a Sunday team and in my first game I let four goals in. As the weeks went by I got better and started playing on a Saturday afternoon as well. I got a new pair of football boots out of our Jackie's catalogue. After a couple of months playing on a Saturday, Sunday and five-a-side during the week, I became a good 'keeper. I would never duck out of a challenge and would pick up loads of bumps and bruises. I was very physical and would love diving at players feet for the ball. One Sunday during a game I went for a 50-50 ball with the oppositions attacker and dived at his feet and won the ball but he screamed out in pain "They've gone" and passed out. He'd had both his legs broken. The ambulance came onto the pitch and stretchered him off as he was 'out'. They called him

Faccinni and he had both his legs in plaster up to his waist for months. One morning a letter arrived from Halifax Town F.C asking for me to go for a trial at their ground. When the day arrived I got my stuff together and went by train, our Kevin came with me. The manager was an ex Hartlepool player called Billy Ayre. I remember stood on the terraces in the seventies watching him play for Hartlepool and there was a song that all the fans would sing and it went "He's here, He's there, He's every fuckin' where, Billy Ayre". There were loads of people at the trial and we were put into teams and played a game. A few minutes into the game I dived at a players feet and won the ball but as I dived I took all the skin off the side of my leg and it was bleeding. It was like diving on gravel and not what you'd expect from a team that was in the football league. I decided then that I was diving no more. A few times I could of won the ball in similar situations but I wouldn't dive because my leg was on fire with the gravel rash. The game ended 2-2 and I never got picked. I knew I wouldn't because I had a shit game. I had played for about eighteen months this time and there were only a couple of games left until the end of this season. When it finished, so did I and hung up my boots for good. I've never played since.

CHAPTER 15

My mother and Ken had lived for a few years in a bungalow. One day when she was cooking the tea, she realised she needed something so she asked Ken to watch the pans while she nipped to the shop which was only round the corner. When she got back the pans were boiling away but there was no Ken? She shouted him but there was no answer. She checked all the rooms and when she walked in the bedroom he was unconscious on the floor. He'd had a massive stroke. Ken would be always on the go, he never sat still. Even if he'd just had a big dinner, five minutes later he'd have to be doing something. He seemed to be full of nervous energy and was like that all his life. He was a keen gardener and had a big greenhouse which he grew , tomatoes and grapes and things. He worked as a joiner from being young apart from a couple of years in the Air Force. My Mam and Ken loved Italy and went there about five times for their holidays. He went into hospital and was totally paralysed down one side due to the stroke. He had to have round the clock care. Me Mam couldn't face putting him in a home so her total life became took over with looking after him. He couldn't do anything for himself, or if he could he stubbornly refused. He wanted me mother to be at his beck and call twenty four hours a day and she was. Every night when she put him to bed he would pull the caffeta off and the bed sheets would be pissed right through and he'd shit himself and I mean every night, seven days a week. All night he'd be shouting to be cleaned up and he had been prescribed the strongest sleeping tablets you could get but they couldn't knock him out. The house started stinking of piss and the sheets and his bed clothes had to be washed everyday, the smell in his bedroom would take your breath away. I'm not kidding when I say he used to ask to be put on the toilet about twenty times a day and 95% of the time me Mam would just get back in the room and he'd shout "Brenda I'm finished, it was only wind". He just wanted attention and to be made a fuss of twenty four hours a day. He would sit in his wheelchair in front of the T.V and he had a bag on the side of his leg with a tube in it what he'd piss in and sometimes when the bag was full he'd turn the valve with his good hand and empty the full bag all over the floor. He was a proper nightmare and I felt sorry for my mother. She got tennis elbow through lifting him all the time. There was a boxing gym not far from where I lived and I knew the trainer Anth. He was a good boxer when he was younger and he was the lad who had that fight with Tank all them years ago. I started going up there a few times a week to hit the bags and get a bit fitter. There was a lad in the gym called Andy Tucker who was an excellent boxer, I can remember many years before when he first started when he was only a nipper. He was in two National finals at Middleweight, N.A.B.C which he lost on points and Junior ABA which he won. He was robbed in the quarter finals of the European championships against an Italian and there was boos at ringside and this was in Poland. I had plenty of respect for Andy, he was a class act. I started sparring with him and gave him some good work and it brought me on a bit. I thought I might as well have a few more fights. His brother Barry was also a good un and I done plenty of rounds with him. Andy had boxed for young England a few times and had just been chosen as their captain against young America. He was in full training and I sparred a lot with him. The T.V cameras came to the gym to interview him and also done a little profile about the club. One night it was shown on a local news programme called Look North. The next night I had a fight lined up but my opponent never turned up because he seen the T.V programme and saw me on the punch bag and said "Fuck that, I'm not fighting him". Andy won his fight against the yank in London.

I was working in a factory for about five months and there was a boxer who worked there and his nickname was Chi, he won the Northern area title as a pro but at the time he was boxing for the Catholic club and they had a show coming up. I got the names of a few top Heavyweights and which clubs they represented and wrote them down on a piece of paper and give it to Chi, I asked him to give it to his trainer who was matchmaking and see if he would get me a fight on the show with any of them. Nothing ever came of it. I was fourteen and a half stone and wanted to fight anybody.

Here's a little story about coincidence. When I was at the factory there was a lad who started and he got put with me and we became friends. His surname was 'Lines' and he said that when he was only a child his father was killed in a street fight in Old Town (an area of Hartlepool).

Years later me mother came back from Glasgow and told me about this Indian picture that was that was on the wall in a bar, she tried to buy it but the manager said he'd had it for years and he'd never seen another one and it wasn't for sale. There was a verse at the bottom of the picture and she wrote it down to show me and kept it.

Years after that my friend George was given two Indian pictures by a bloke who moved in a few doors from him. He brought one of the pictures up for me to keep and me mother said "I've seen that picture somewhere before", then she realised it was the same as the one in the bar in Glasgow. She found the piece of paper with the verse on it and checked it with the one on the picture and it was the same verse.

The bloke who gave George the pictures had been to prison years before for manslaughter after he killed a man in a street fight in Old Town. The man he killed was called 'Lines' and was the father of the lad I used to work with at the factory. If that's not coincidence I don't know what is and about six weeks after he gave George them pictures, the bloke had a heart attack and died.

Anth the boxing coach was a bouncer and he asked me if they got stuck, would I fancy doing a bit and I said yes. I started working the door with Anth, Brian, Peter and Rick. It was a very busy pub with two floors and a disco upstairs. I learned the ropes from the lads, how to be fair but firm, always in control and never flustered and how to control the crowds and queues. We had a few fights but generally things went fine and I had some good times working with them for about four months.

I fought this big guy at a boxing show; he'd had eight fights and won seven. His only loss was avenged by a knockout. A couple of cars full of lads from the gym and a couple of lads from off the door came to watch me. At the show I could see the look on people's faces when they said "Are you fighting him" and I said "Yes". I think they were concerned for my safety. He was built like a brick shithouse and looked very impressive, he had an air of confidence about him which I was determined to shatter. On my walk to the Ring I couldn't wait to get in because by this time I was right up for it and just wanted to fight. As the bell went he came straight me and tried to put me away, he'd jumped on me and was looking for a quick finish. I took some good shots from him and then I opened up with my arsenal and we traded toe to toe. I had a burning desire in me to win and started to get him on the back foot when I put him down with the muck spreader right hand. He got up and took the count and the ref waved us to continue. I went after him like a predator and was all over him, lefts and rights smashing into his head. By now his face was covered in blood and he was about to go down when the ref stepped in and stopped it. It was very explosive while it lasted and the crowd loved it. I went to the hospital the next day and was told I had a burst eardrum. We offered them a return fight but they refused. I had my eyes set on the ABA title and was training hard for it.

When the day of the ABA's arrived I was a little excited as this was what I'd been waiting for. We got to Gateshead Leisure Centre and went to get weighed in. The official in charge said the weighing in of boxers was over. A heated argument ensued as he wouldn't let me step on the scales. He said that every club had been sent a letter saying that boxers had to be weighed in by 7p.m, it was now 7-15p.m. It was the first time we'd heard of such a letter but he still wouldn't let me step on the scales and any dreams I had of winning the ABA title ended right there and I was really gutted. We found out that there was a letter, but it wasn't sent to the coach like it should of been, it was sent to the social club and the treasurer read it and stuck it in the drawer and forgot to tell anyone about it. When I heard this I felt like smashing his face in. What made it worse was that I really believe I would have gone all the way. A silly incident like that destroyed a dream. That done my plug in and I started to drift away from boxing.

My mother had been looking after Ken 24 hours a day for two years and was at the end of her tether. She asked if me and Gail would move in and help her out, it was a big house so we said yes and we all lived under the same roof. Ken was as bad as ever wanting attention 24-7. One day Gail and me mam were out shopping when the day centre bus pulled up and brought Ken back. He went there two days a week. As soon as he got in he was moaning to be put on the toilet because he said he was busting. I told him it'll be wind but he insisted it wasn't. I said "Look I'll put you on but I'm not getting you off, you have to stay there until my mother gets in". He said ok. I wheeled him to the toilet and put him on and left him. Two minutes later he was shouting to be off after another false alarm as it was only wind. I said "You are staying on the bog until me Mam comes in so stop moaning" and closed the door and ignored his pleas. He was sat there for an hour. The family have laughed over it a few times. I bought a puppy, a Staffordshire bull terrier bitch and called her Cassie, she was lovely and the kids adored her. The kids gave me chicken pox and I was a total mess. I'd never had them before but when I got them I was covered from head to toe. If I had a pound for every pock I'd of been a millionaire because there was that many. Me mother bought the kids a Kylie Minogue video and they had it on from morning 'till night for months. We had a stair lift in for Ken and the kids loved to go on it when they went to bed. The kids developed little wart like things on their eyelids, neck, arms and hands. I can't remember the official name for them but they went into Sunderland Infirmary overnight and had them cauterised and they never got them again, the kids called them flumps. I'd always take them out to the park and swings and they loved it. Willy Wonka got some hammer in the video recorder as well. I was a proper father and it felt great, those times were very precious to me. I got our Jill as much as I could so they would grow up as brother and sisters, Jill was getting taller and prettier all the time. A chip off the old block.

CHAPTER 16

When I was younger there was this bloke who used to work the doors and I'd hear stories about him fighting and he was supposedly handy. He became a pub landlord, the bouncers there were run by an agency called A1 and run by the two Mick's, Blackwood and Sorby. He told them he wanted me on the door because he knew his pub would be in safe hands which was very nice of him to say. I went to work there and the two Mick's came to see me and we shook hands. They both said they knew my face, I definitely knew Sorby's as he had a nasty reputation and was not to be messed with. He was battling most of the time and had just had a fight with another hard man and bit his nose off, he took no prisoners. When I got to know him he was a great bloke and best man at my wedding. Two of us worked the door at this boozer, there was a disco and bar upstairs and just a bar with a pool table downstairs. Charlie was my partner, he'd been to prison for violence and shoving guns down people's throats and that. The first time I ever seen him was on the caravan site when I was a kid, he had relatives on there and had a reputation as a nutcase even then. He wore a steel plate around his stomach when he was on the door so if anyone hit him there they would bust their hands. You couldn't see it under his clothes neither but it was there. We'd have a few sociable drinks and a good chin wag and everything would go alright. When gangs of lads came in they were told in no uncertain terms that they'd better behave themselves, when you tell them like that it either goes one way or the other and most of them lose their bottle when they see you mean every word. This bloke came in one night and had a bust up with his woman, he started to smash all the glasses that were stacked up waiting to be washed and must have smashed about sixty glasses. I could hear all the smashing as I came from the toilet, Charlie was downstairs checking on the bar. The geezer went to leave the place but had to get past me to go through the door. The whole pub were watching him, he was marching straight towards me with a big snarl on his face. I stood in the way to block him and he threw a punch at me, I slipped it and snapped out a straight right which landed smack on the button. He was on the deck groaning and covered in blood and all the fight had gone out of him. Right at that moment Charlie returned and picked the guy up and took him in the toilets to be cleaned up. My hand is throbbing by now so I looked down and there's a big gash in my knuckles and claret is pissing out. I'd knocked his front teeth out and they'd stuck in my hand, I still have the scar today. A few weeks later I got banged up for it, he never went to the police until two weeks later. Somebody had put him wise about getting compensation; anyway the crown prosecution kicked it into touch. It's amazing how many arseholes there are like that bloke out there. The manager went to run another boozer and Charlie packed in so I was working with a big mush called Tony. I'd seen his face somewhere before but couldn't think where, it turned out he was my cousin as his real father was my uncle Jimmy. We had a photo of him as a kid in one of our albums and he'd never changed, that's why I knew his face. We had some good nights on the door, that was when "Pump Up The Jam" and all that were big in the charts.

Gail was working at a chip shop everyday and always going here and there with this one and that one. I was sure she was having an affair but I wasn't bothered about her, them kids were my life and I loved them to bits. I wanted everything to be as normal as possible for them and they couldn't of been any happier. We had birthday parties for them both (Donna Oct, Terry June) and we'd invite their school friends and relatives and me mother would always have a big spread on for them, Sandwiches, Cakes, Pop, Crisps, Jelly, Ice Cream, a birthday cake with candles on and there'd always be games like pass the parcel and musical chairs. There would be plenty of lager for the adults and we had some great times. An old friend of me Mam's called Mary always called in with sweets for the kids and our dog Cassie was always licking the salt of her feet. I'd take Cassie out for a five mile walk everyday with my mate George and his dog. We put some miles in together. One time we drank a bottle of whiskey between us and took the dogs for a walk while we were drunk. I had a feeling Gail was being unfaithful and it was just a matter of time before we split up and but it was going to kill me to lose the kids so I kept my mouth shut for their sake. They were doing well in school and had a happy home and I didn't want any unrest for them but I also didn't want to be a fool, there's an old saying "What's good for the goose is good for the gander" so I started seeing a young lass who came in the pub, a bonnie girl who was only eighteen. I was seeing her for about six months, by day I was a full time father but at night I turned into Banana Man. One time I made arrangements to go back to this lasses house, she said the windows would be open if her boyfriend was out. After work I went round and they were open so I knocked on the door and within ten minutes we were in bed. She called me Merlin because she said I was a wizard between the sheets. She said "Stop I can hear a noise". Her boyfriend had returned and was stood on the stairs listening. Talk about getting caught red handed, I was caught red ended. He walked back downstairs and went in the room. I think the only reason he never came in the bedroom was because I left my coat in the front room and he had a look of it and thought "He's a big cunt". I put my clothes on and went downstairs. The boyfriend said "Alright Richy". I said "Alright Johnny, I didn't know she was your bird or I wouldn't of fucked her". That didn't go down too well. I put my coat on and left. I didn't know his full name, I only knew him as Johnny and I'd never seen him for years so when she said his name at the pub I never knew him. I saw her a few days later walking down Church Street with two black eyes.

I was wanted elsewhere so I worked in loads of different pubs. I worked all the roughest bars in town, all the troubled spots. On bank holidays I would be guaranteed at least three fights and that was on a bad day. I kept myself to myself then and when there was trouble I'd be straight in to sort it, sometimes I'd chin a few because that's the only language some people understand. I worked with numerous lads, Andy, Philly, Trev, Marcel, Kenny, Eddie, Martin, Mick Sorby and many more. I had fought some tough cookies but the first real hard man I fought was when I was on the door. This man could fight and was in his prime, strong as a bull and about seventeen stone. He'd had a grievance with the doormen of a pub one night and went off his head and knocked them out. Then he just went from pub to pub knocking bouncers out and the word got straight round he was heading in our direction. We were called to a pub what had our doormen on, we were told there was fighting. It was him but he'd already left. We went in and the bouncers were smashed to bits, shirts ripped off, teeth knocked out, claret and glass everywhere. I flew back to my pub before he got there and stood at the entrance, it was chucking out time when he turned up. There was anticipation in the air in the boozer. I was with Blackie whose doormen he'd been flattening and by the time he reached us ten bouncers had been pummelled by him. Blackie started to fight with him straight away giving it his all but then started to take a beating so I dragged the geezer off and threw him to the ground. A load of people were already in the street and plenty more were coming out the pubs. I knew this was it and I was ready. He got up and stood in the middle of the road and said "I want to fight you now". My adrenalin was going and I obliged him. I walked over and he came to me. I moved in close and hit him with two right uppercuts which both landed one after the other, Bang, Bang. He was still on his feet but backed up and then I hit him with a right, left, right and he went down. I booted him in the head and turned around and walked fast into the pub away from the scene. Everyone in the place was buzzing at how quick I done him. After we got everyone out we had a lock in and he came back and was banging on the windows to be in. He was waving a knife about and we wouldn't let him in so he stabbed all the tyres of the cars outside. Not long after that we settled our differences and became friends.

Every Sunday I'd travel to different Spiritualist Churches. It gave me spiritual enlightenment and I enjoyed getting away from the hustle and bustle of the doors. I did that for two years and seen countless mediums, some good and some bad. I got some good messages at the churches, now and again I'd have a private sitting with a good clairvoyant and they'd give me proof. I often wake up during the night and most times I find it hard to go back to sleep. One night when I woke up I seen the spirit of a young girl stood at the side of the bed. It startled me for a couple of seconds but things like this have happened to me on a number of occasions over the years. I'd say she was about eight years old and had long dark hair that came past her shoulders and was wearing an old fashioned school uniform and white hat, just like the Saint Trinians. She never spoke to me she just stared and I felt a nice peaceful energy coming from her, I also sensed another spirit in the room which I couldn't see but I think it was somebody with the child. After what seemed like 20 seconds but was really only about 10, they were both gone. I haven't a clue who they were or what they wanted.

I went back to the Boys Welfare for a few months and by then I was weighing fifteen and a half stone. I had some good hard sparring sessions there. I always liked it at the Welfare, there was just something about it and it was always a challenge when I got in the ring because all the young guns I sparred with would give me their best shots all the time.

I started going to a kickboxing gym because I knew the trainer. Every session started with a run and I would always trail in last. I noticed they were brilliant with their kicks but not that clever with their hands so I'd get in the ring and spar with them, just hands and no feet. The purpose of this was to bring them on a bit with their punching and I'd tell them they could hit me as hard as they can while I pulled mine. I'd do eight rounds straight off and they'd say "How come you can do that when I'm fitter than you but shattered after two". It was all down to one word: Experience. I'd also do a couple skipping and two or three on the heavy bag. The trainer took me for a few sessions of kicking and was keen for me to have a few fights and then enter the British championships. He said I had what it takes. I wasn't really into all that kicking and declined his offer.

CHAPTER 17

After four years of my mother looking after him, Ken had to finally go into a home because of me Mam's ill health. Her elbows were shattered through lifting him and she had Osteoporosis. She even had to get an electric tin opener because she broke her wrist in two places while opening a tin.

Me and Gail finally split up, it had been on the cards for a long time and we only stayed together because of the kids. I'd been prepared for a split for months but it doesn't matter how much you prepare, when you lose your kids it hits you harder than any physical blow. I went upstairs and broke my heart. A strong man cries, it's the weak man who holds back his tears. He thinks "People will discover my weakness if they see or hear me cry". When you don't cry, it all builds up inside you and that causes breakdowns which can emotionally destroy you. You feel much better if you can cry because it releases a lot of built up tension, crying in private is the best option for the so called 'Hard Man'. I never saw the children for about six months and I told myself I'd never be put through that pain again ever. It affected me a bit because I don't like to get too close to anyone and there's even a little distance there with my kids. I love my kids more than anything and have an unlimited amount of feelings for them but I never tell them.

I got friendly with a girl from Middlesbrough called Heather. She was a lovely lass and I even went to the pictures with her to see 'Dances With Wolves'. I went out round Middlesbrough with her a few times drinking and nightclubbing. Lee Duffy was the big name in the town but I never bumped into him which I thought was strange. She came to my pub one night with her cousin and I set up a blind date for her with my mate Rob. On the night we went through to Boro for a drink and the blind date I was teasing Rob saying "She's not up to much but she'll do for you" and things like that, winding him up. Anyway they turned up and Rob was over the moon with her and visa versa. To cut a long story short he moved in with her for about five years and they had two kids. I got crabbs off a girl and passed them on to Heather. One night she came in the pub shouting "Thanks for the dose of fucking crabbs", she was shouting loud to show me up but I stayed cool and said "It's ok your quite welcome". I never seen her again, I wonder why? I was also seeing a lass at the same time called Samantha but somehow she never caught them, the cream must of worked. I went to the skills centre at Billingham to do a bricklaying course. It was five days a week and eight hours a day and the gaffa used to shout at all the lads but wouldn't dare say nowt to me. After six weeks I'd had enough and chucked it.

I started to work at a pub on the seafront; it was a karaoke bar and was full to the brim all the time. I was working with a lad called Vul and after we got everyone out the pub we'd go to the nightclub which was upstairs and work there until two. Vul's relations would come to the club and we had some good nights, there were even relatives of his that came up from Leeds. The manager told us one night that the owners were getting Lee Duffy over to pay him protection money to look after their clubs and he'd be over next week. That week there was a couple of naughty looking lads in from Boro checking the place out. They came back a week later when Duffy was supposed to be coming. Another week later the manager said "Lee Duffy is coming tomorrow night". He never turned up again because he was entertaining friends in Boro and later that same night he was stabbed to death. Vul got nine months for assault so Dickie was brought in to work with me, then Andy and Lee. It was usually a canny night and the only trouble was from drunken families. One time when there was a big row and there was any amount at it, a geezer faked a heart attack, the ambulance wheeled him out with a oxygen mask on. Andy said to me he didn't think that bloke was for real and sure enough we found out later that he'd faked it.

One night at a Spiritualist church a medium was giving an old woman a message and during it he said "I have Dick here who wants to be known" and the old woman said "Yes, I can take Dick". I nearly fell of my seat laughing. There was only me in the congregation who saw the funny side of it, nobody else batted an eye lid. With my sense of humour my sides were splitting and I couldn't stop so I went outside for some fresh air and to sort myself out.

I got interested in the American Indian when I first started going to Ruby's philosophy nights. She'd talk about them and how spiritual they were. How they were so in tune with nature and lived off the land. I read a few books about them and their way of life and got hooked, it really appealed to me. My favourite tribe are the Lakota Sioux. The Indian was the first true American. The history of how they fought for their country is written in blood. Their god was the sun, their church was the great outdoors, their only book was nature and they knew all of it's pages.

The nights that I wasn't working I was out drinking with the lads. I took this bewer (lass) home one night I'd known for years, I'd never had anything to do with her before and she wasn't that good looking. Our Tank picked me up the next morning and was shocked, He'd known her years as well and he said "What the fuck are you doing with her she's a whore, I'm surprised at you, She's had more cock ends than weekends". I knew that already but when you are out every night you just go with the flow. I was single and if there was any loose skirt at the end of the night that looked half decent you don't turn your nose up at it, know what I mean.

This Irish bloke came to the town after doing six years for a stabbing. He was about 6ft 3in and started working the doors that I used to work and I got to know him. He wanted a reputation for some reason and started playing up to me. I had a quiet word with him and told him to get in the toilets if he wants to fight me. He had a good look in my eyes and realised I was serious and said 'No'. I found out he'd only been out of prison a couple of weeks when he carved someone else up in Carlisle and was waiting to go to Crown Court. He got on with a girl and wanted her to marry him quickly so it looked good at court making out he'd met the right woman and had settled down. You can bet they never got a set of knives as a wedding present. Five days after they were married he got five years.

I started to work at this place in the town centre; it was jam packed all the time and there was fighting most nights. It was two places in one. There was a bar and a D.J downstairs and at the side you walked up about forty stairs and there was a bar and disco, dance floor, D.J and all that what we looked after as well. I knew before I started to work there that I would be fighting all the time and I was right, I was there for about eighteen months and seen plenty of doormen come and go in that time. My first night they tell me about this bloke who comes in every week who won't see his drinks off and makes them look a bit silly because he loves an audience. Well it was late and there was only a few left to get out, it was always a headache getting people out when they're full of alcohol. There were some lads stood round some of the doormen, they were fucking about and playing up because they had this prick with them. Every time he was asked to "See your drink off", he'd pick it up and wave 'bye bye' to his drink to 'See it off'. I walk up and tell him to finish his drink or I'm taking it away. I don't like people taking the piss so you have to be firm with them. The prick just sat there smirking at me, I reached over and grabbed his pint and poured it over his huge head. Before he could move I smack him with a straight right and flatten the prick. His mates shouted that they didn't want any trouble and they all left. They took him to the hospital were they found out I'd broke his nose not to mention his ego. Suffice to say he never tried his little tricks again. He did consider pressing charges but then thought better of it. Now if it was him who did that to me, I would never even give it a thought to get the police involved. That was the trouble with working the doors, you were always in a no win situation. The forty stairs that led to the disco, one night I had a fight right in the middle of them. The lad knew me from when I was young and thought he could take me so we met on the middle stair and went at it. I was trying to get my footing so I could get some leverage but it was awkward. Once I landed he went down and was laid across the stairs when I cracked a couple more into him. The doormen at the top of the stairs were shouting "Richy, he's had enough", but I knew that already. I worked with plenty of good lads there, Wally, Rob, Vul, Eric, Podey, Mick, Paulie, Frankie, Alan, Dickie, Andy, Nick and loads more. The lass I was with at the time was the lass Tank told me to stay away from or my dick would fall off. She worked in a nightclub and I'd always be in with the lads getting loads of free drink. I had loads of fights in that nightclub as well. I won't say her name because I despise her. On one occasion I was talking with this woman, nothing in it just talking. I notice over the other side of the room there's a bloke throwing his arms about in a threatening manner and shouting something I couldn't hear because of the noise. There were two of them, a big one and a small one who was doing all the shouting. I thought to myself "Is he talking to me" and look around and realise he is. We lock eyes and I point to myself and mouth "Are you talking to me?" he nods 'Yes' and continues with the obscenities. I excused myself to the woman and made my way over. I stopped to ask my friend Buller to watch my back, the thing is people like this can't be talked to so I wasn't going to mess around. I hit the mouthy one with a right, left, right, smack on the chin and he was unconscious before he hit the deck. I turned to the big guy and off he shot like Linford Christie. I caught him and hit him with a right which didn't catch him properly but still put him down. Fear was keeping him awake as he was scrambling under the tables to hide from me. As the bouncers arrived I was putting the boot into him without much success. The doormen couldn't revive the other one and after about ten minutes the ambulance arrived. We were on the top floor of the club and the doormen had to carry him down the stairs and he was still unconscious. At the hospital they wired his jaw up and he drank through a straw for a couple of months, I can't remember how many places his jaw was broke in. The big guy told someone that the punch he was hit with was like being hit with a hammer. From what I could gather the smaller one had been going out with the woman I was talking to for a couple of years. The big one had a reputation as a fighter. The smaller one thought his mate would help him out of the shit but of course the shit hit the fan. Buller said to me "What did you want me to watch your back for? You were having a fucking laugh".

Another time I was at the bar getting a drink and this geezer is stood at the bar with a ciggie in his mouth trying his best to look 'Rock Hard'. He takes a drag and points in my face and says "Don't I know you" and he's looking snake eyed at me like a gangster. I stood in front of him and said " I don't know, but they call me Richy Horsley" and then Bang, I hit him with a left hook. He was stood there leaning against the bar and staring into space, knocked out standing up. I spoke again but never got a response so I walked away and left the drink. When he came round he went to the hospital and I was told by a few people his jaw was broke in two places. Another night I was talking to these two sisters who I hadn't seen for a few years. One of their ex boyfriends was hovering around looking for trouble and he thought I was trying to tap one of them up. He wanted a fight with me but I was talking so I pretended I was scared of him and said no. He grew another foot and his chest came out another six inches. When I finished my drink and said "See ya, nice talking to ya" to the sisters, I went up to him and said "Yeah, let's fight" and dropped him with the first punch. He was fucked but I put the boot in as well because he was a cheeky cunt. The bouncers came over and picked him up and threw him out the club.

CHAPTER 18

I remember one New Years Eve, I'd been working since noon and when I had finished I was the worse for wear. I'd had a drink and a few fights throughout the day, sometimes I can remember fights and sometimes I can't. I was with the lass from the nightclub and by the time we got to her brother's house it was about four in the morning and I was pissed. Her thirteen year old daughter was sleeping there and when I was going to the bog there was a commotion on the landing. This Cockney lad was trying to get in the bedroom where the young girl was and there was some carry on so I clipped him and staggered into the toilet while he was escorted downstairs. I was in the bathroom when I can here all hell breaking loose and the Cockney lads pal was Big Bri from our town and he was going berserk screaming he wanted me in the garden. I didn't want to fight him because I was pissed but I had too. Big Bri was a lunatic and had natural strength, he was as strong as an ox and people were frightened to death of him. As soon as I got in the garden, BANG, he hit me with a cracking right and I went down, my legs are like jelly and I don't know where I am. He got on top of me and I couldn't even lift my hands up. He started letting the punches go and they were smashing into my face with sickening thuds. Everybody was watching but nobody dared say anything. While I was getting beat to within an inch of my life the Cockney lad booted me in the head about five times. I remember thinking "I wish I was sober". I thought he was going to kill me because he kept smashing away and I was slipping away but I was telling myself to stay with it and after what seemed an eternity, he got off. The only reason the stopped was because he thought I was dead, I nearly was. He had a couple of rings on and I was cut to ribbons, the flesh on my nose was cut wide open and my eyes were both cut open above and under. I was in a right state. I couldn't see out of one eye so two days later I went to the Eye Infirmary and they said the eyeball was grazed were the pupil was but it would heal. I stayed away from bouncing until I healed up. It was all over the town that I was done easy and there was a new kid on the block. He revelled in the glory and told the story of the fight time after time. It was all pats on the back and free drinks for the new king and I was told he was going round like he was King Kong. A few months passed and I got a phone call telling me the Cockney lad was in the nightclub. I went straight down and got a pint and one of the doormen let me stand on the fire exit back stairs. He told him he wanted a word because he believed he'd been smoking dope. The door opened and he walked through and the bouncer shut the door. I dropped my pint as I went for him and slipped in it, as I fell down the stairs I grabbed hold of him and he came with me. I let him have it to head and body and he was squealing like a pig. I left him outside the fire doors at the back of the club laid in a heap. I was glad I got hold of that wanker, one down one to go. Next in line was a return with King Kong. About a month after that I thought "its judgement day" and knew it was time to fight Big Bri, he'd had his glory and if he wanted to keep my title he was going to have to kill me. I went to the club were he was. I had my back up, Ryao, Vul, Eric and Mick in case of foul play. I didn't go in but I looked through the windows and the big twat's in there and he's got his back to me. That's when the butterflies start in the stomach. I had been constantly thinking about the first fight "was it the drink or was he the better man". I had to find out. I waited over the road and he came out and shouted "so you want another good hiding do yah?", he's very confident. He comes at me and throws a big right but I'm ready for it and block it. I put a couple of big shots on him and he went down. I get on top of him and smash him to bits and break both my hands. He was making funny noises and was choking on his own blood and when I got off him I thought I'd killed him. He was rushed to hospital and it was touch and go for a while but luckily he pulled through. I was back on top and people used to call me Crazy Horse because of my name being Horsley and my own interest in the American Indian. I was having a couple of street fights a week and it seemed like people were coming from all over to have a go because word spread like wild fire about the fighting. I got locked up a few times but I always had witnesses and so I was never charged. One Sunday night I was out with the lass

from the nightclub, I'd been working the pubs and clubs and street fighting all the time so I promised myself a trouble free night. We went to a place I used to work a few years before and I got between two guys at the bar. One of them said "Who the fuck are you pushing". I bit my tongue and ignored him. Then he said "Do you want chew" (chew is trouble). I said 'No' and he replied "You better not if you know what's good for you". I got the drinks and went to the other side of the room and all the time this stupid twat was going through my head. He kept looking over and saying something to his pals. I thought "That's it; the quiet night is out the window".
I weighed up the situation, there was three of then and just me. I went and stood by the door, you had to go through it to leave. After what seemed like ages they decided to leave. I stood in front of the door blocking it. The prick with all the mouth was wandering what was going on. "I do want chew" I said and lifted him out his boots with a big right and the wanker didn't know what hit him. He was sleeping on the floor with blood coming from a deep gash. His two mates turned white and shit themselves, they didn't want it. A woman was screaming and the manager told me to leave before the ambulance came so I did. Vul's cousin Eddie ran a boozer and it never mattered what time of the day or night it was we could always get a drink there. We had some good sessions in there that went on for days. My mate Eric reminded me recently that after some trouble one night everyone went back there and started pulling things from their coats and put them on a table, the table ended up piled high with coshes, axes, knuckledusters, machetes, baseball bats etc. I thought the trouble was over with the bloke with all the mouth, he told people that I'd hit him with a glass ashtray. Why he couldn't tell the truth god knows. I went to this pub one day to sort some trouble out but the lad I wanted to see had pissed off. Who was sat there with all his pals, yes the mouthy twat. It was like walking into an enemy's camp. As I was outside walking away I hear "Oi you", I turn round and he's standing there with a load of his mates behind him. He shouts "Who do you think you are", "Don't ever come here to sort chew out in my pub". I ignored him as there was too many of them. I went straight

over to Eddie's boozer and there was a few of the lads in, as look would have it some friends from Boro were there as well so we jumped in a couple of motors and went over. We went in and the prick was on his own. His pals must have known I'd be back and fucked off. He wouldn't come in the car park to fight because my friends were there, not even just us two. He starts raising his voice so I thought 'Fuck this' and gave it to him. I broke three of his ribs with a body punch and he had internal bleeding. The barman told me later that when the ambulance carted him off, he thought the geezer was dead. He never came back for more but he was going to give this other hard man two grand to do me over. This guy was twenty stone and strong as a bull and had a reputation; it was all over the town. It was set for a certain night and I went to the nightclub with the lads, you could feel the electricity in the air. I was in one room and he was in the other. The head doorman was begging me not to fight in there but I told him to Fuck off and he walked away with his tail between his legs. I had a couple of drinks and said "It's time". We went in the room and a lad I know said "He's just left; he bottled it at the last minute". That was a big comedown because I'd been psyching myself up for him. A few weeks later I seen him in the night club and stood not far from him eyeballing him and he shook his head to say 'No' and turned away from me. Them days I was just like the Robert DeNiro character in the film Raging Bull and had the same mannerism. The lass from the night club didn't help because she was always causing trouble for me but I couldn't see it. I was like a clockwork mouse, all you had to do was put the key in and wind me up. There was a local geezer, a well respected hard man who had fought for money called Davo. He had fought bare knuckle and had beaten some very good men in street fights in bars and car parks and to my knowledge had never lost. I'd known of him for years as a fighting man, they say he had gypsy blood in him. He certainly had a touch of something in him because he was shady skinned. He had jet black shoulder length hair he sometimes wore in a ponytail, wore a bit of gold, tattoos, wagga dot tattoo on his cheek, get the picture. Nobody wanted chew with him. There was another hard man in the town called T.R who thought he could beat anyone in the UK, anyway T.R fought Davo twice and got knocked out twice. The lass I was with said Davo kept coming in the nightclub trying to tap her up. She said "I'll tell Richy" and he'd say "What can Richy do with me, he can do nowt with me", "I'll beat him easy" and all the rest of it. When I got told and I was stewing with it for a week. I was working in a bar on Saturday afternoons because it got all the riff raff in and they needed someone in there who these people respected. They knew if there was any trouble in there when I was working, the trouble causes were the ones going to the outpatients. Davo and his pals got in there on a Saturday afternoon. I took the afternoon off because I wanted to get the job done with him and get out. He always had a crowd with him and the bar had lots of rough guys in as well. I went with Vul and Andy, it wasn't a secret there was going to be trouble and no doubt a few people were sat in prime spots waiting for the action. A description of me as I was waiting for him, I was 6ft 1in, 16 and a half stone (solid), wearing an England shell suit and trainers, I had a skinhead and a stubble. I said to Vul "I'll wait until he goes to the bar and go over and offer him outside", Vul said "Nah, just get stuck in as soon as you see him". I was toying with what to do and decided to get stuck in. One of his mates comes in and I knew he was close, then a couple more and then some more, until finally he comes in last of all. I walk straight over as he's coming through the door. He knew I was coming for him so as I throw the right hand he tried to slip it but BANG I catch him with it. He hit the deck and I must of caught him with a good un because there's claret all over him. He's dazed and looking up at me with blood pissing out of a nasty cut as I bend over him and say "Stop messing with my woman". Then I hit him with a peach of a left hook on the side of the jaw and his eyes rolled and he went out like a light. He lost a few teeth and wet himself. I look up at his mates and none of them would look me in the face, I shout "Come on then who wants it?" and none of them wanted to know. I walked out the back door and jumped in a motor and left, then people started shouting about what they were gonna do to me and a couple of knives were pulled out with dickheads saying

"He's gonna get this". Then the ambulance turned up and took Davo away.

There were loads of lies going around the town because he had never tasted defeat before. Shit things like I hit him from behind and ran to the police station demanding protection. What kind of people are they who make lies up like that. To make matters worse, a lot of people believed the rumours because to them he was unbeatable and their hero. It was talked about all over town and the place was buzzing. Then it turned into revenge. It was like people were wanting revenge for the killing of Custer, after all I was Crazy Horse. People were saying Davo was gonna kill me and the town were talking about the return fight and how he'd murder me. Davo went into training for eight weeks to prepare for the second fight while his friends tried to get the scalp of Crazy Horse. People were betting money on the outcome and T.R had a bet with a few that Davo would win, probably as he'd been done twice by him. There was a friend of Davo's who used to run the doors in the town and was a bit of a tough guy, he was also well connected. He was in the nightclub full of Dutch courage and being a total arsehole but I ignored him. The next week he done exactly the same only with more front so I thought "I've had enough of this". He was a big man, all twenty five stones of him, but a fat fucker who thought he was a right handful. I shouted "Oi fat cunt, you're getting on my fucking tits". He put his drink down and came straight for me wanting blood, he got blood but it was his own. As soon as he got near me I hit him with a powerful right hand and left hook and as they landed I broke both hands, his huge head was like hitting a brick wall. He went down in front of the bar on the tiled floor BANG and broke both knees with the weight of him. My hands were in pain but I kept punching and knocked him out. The doormen wouldn't come near me but the manageress of the club was on my back screaming. She later told people she thought she had a death on her hands. He went to hospital with two broken knees, a broken jaw and got stitched up like a road map. He brought it all on himself, it was him who wanted it not me. Then there was another load of lies flying round and what he told people really takes the biscuit. He said there was me and two lads and one done Kung Fu. The Kung Fu bloke swept his legs from under him and the other lad smashed his legs with an iron bar and then I finished him off. His girlfriend who was with him backed him up totally. What a fucking fairytale they came up with, why couldn't they tell the truth. Probably because the truth hurts. So more bad publicity went round the town about me. He and his family were well connected so they got in touch with one of the hardest men money can buy called Viv Graham and told him the cock and bull story. There were rumours that he was coming and people were saying watch for this and watch for that. I was working the doors so I wasn't hard to find and told people I wasn't going anywhere. Then someone pulled me up whose name I'll leave anonymous and he said "I've had Viv Graham on the phone asking me about you, he wanted to know what happened with Philly", I said "What did you tell him", he said "I told him the truth and also told him you were a nice bloke who wouldn't take a liberty". Viv said he had a feeling they weren't telling the truth and left it at that but like I always say "There are always two sides to every story". Philly's brother Frankie is the only decent one out of the full family. Another one of their clan came in the nightclub and started being disrespectful to me so I set about him as well and wiped him out and he was taken to hospital by ambulance and was in for a few days, he got any amount of stitches. I still had two broken hands when I give him it. I was thinking to myself "Will any of these dickheads ever learn". A couple of dykes I'd known for years came up to me in the club and one said "I hear you're fighting Davo again, aren't you frightened?". I said "Am I fuck, he's the one who's getting knocked out not me". They were looking at me with disbelief. Some blokes got together with Davo so they could give him an alibi because they were putting a plan together to have me gunned down. Davo told them he wanted nothing to do with it and that he would sort his trouble out with me himself, fair play to him. That meeting was top secret but I still found out about it. A geezer who I barely knew was torturing me to go to this pub one night for a lock in, he went on and on trying to get me there but I wouldn't go. He went on too much and I was suspicious about it. I found out that Davo and all my other enemies were in there and this cheeky cunt tried to deliver me on a plate. My pal Mick Sorby seen him in a pub and knocked him cold with one punch. There was a stench in the air because the geezer had shit himself and I mean literally shit himself.

CHAPTER 19

I got a job for a couple of months installing heavy electric cables, it was contracting work with a local firm and the job was at Port Glasgow in Scotland. There was a knock on the door and when I opened it, Bernie the lad I knocked out a few years before, was stood there and said "Alright Richy" and we got in the van and headed off. We became good friends. On the way there the radio in the van was playing the number one hit record 'End of the Road' by Boys To Men, they must of played it three times before we got there. We stayed there and done the job in seven days. When we got back we were put on a job at Wallsend installing the cable for an oil module that was going out to sea. It was just what I needed to get away from all the chew (trouble). Then one Saturday afternoon the phone rang, it was Davo and he was ready to fight. I told him I'd been out all night, which I had, and to phone me back at tea time. I rested up until tea time and he phoned me back. He wanted to fight straight away but I said it will have to be seven o'clock and he said ok and we arranged to meet in a pub car park. It was bonfire night and I was planning to let my fireworks go off in the car park. My mate Andy picked me up and took me there, when we arrived he was waiting. I spotted a couple of his relatives dotted about to relay news of the fight back to people. I got out the car and went over and we shook hands, he said "I've got to fight you Richy, it was a bit fast last time". He was trained up for this and he looked impressive in a white vest. I took my coat off and we squared up. We were stood there and he was waiting for me to make the first move. I threw a light feeler and he came under it and grabbed me round the waist to take me to the floor, the sneaky twat. We landed on our sides and I was stronger and got on top. I tried to smash his head off the floor but his neck muscles were too strong and he said "You dirty bastard". I got my hands free and hit him with two heavy shots. My punches were meant to go through his head and my hands were bleeding as my knuckles had little stones in them from the gravel in the car park and he said he'd had enough. I wasn't satisfied and hit him twice more and he was

fucked and all smashed up. I couldn't hit him anymore or it might of been serious so I got up and as I'm walking away I hear him shout me "Richy, Richy". I walk back and look at him laid there covered in blood and he can't get up. He said "Richy, you can't leave me laid here like this", So I thought "Fair do's" and pick him up and take him to his car. I'm a fair man and I don't take liberties, once a man is done he's done and that's it. If I had got beat fair, I'd come back to fight again. If I still got beat I would have shaken his hand and admitted he was the better man. I have got a lot of respect for Davo and the way he came back to fight one on one like a man. We have been friends ever since.
I went to work on the Monday and was in severe pain with my hands so I asked the gaffa to take me to the hospital at Hartlepool and he did and went back to work. On the way in, a jeep pulled up and it was T.R and a few cronies and he asked what was the matter. I told him I was getting my hands checked after damaging them knocking Davo out again. He didn't know the result and you should of seen his face, he was gutted because he had money on Davo to win. I don't think he believed me, he wanted to know everything, a blow by blow account.
As the job at Wallsend was winding down, one lad every week was laid off. When it was my turn I said "See ya" and got my gear and walked off the job. It was opening time so I had few pints and had no money left so I started walking home. I walked through the pedestrian part of the Tyne Tunnel and along the A19 towards Hartlepool which was forty miles away. After a few hours I went in a garage and the bloke let me reverse the charges and I left a message on someone's answer machine. I got picked up at night about five miles outside Hartlepool, when I got home and tried to get out the car my legs had seized up.
We were out celebrating Vul's birthday one night, it was about 8-30p.m. We walked into this pub and no one spotted him but me, it was Big Bri, the lad who I had the two brutal near death fights with. He was with his woman and another couple. I kept it to myself and pretended I never seen him. They finished their drinks and I watched

them leave. As we left Vul was chatting to the bouncers and I was about the fifth one out the door. As soon as I get on the street BANG I take a massive right hand from Bri, he'd waited over the road and when he saw my pals coming out he started running over and his timing was perfect. There was a blinding light before my eyes and I don't know what's happened. My head's spinning as he hits me again, I fly back against the window and he put another on my chin. If there was nothing behind me I think I'd of gone down. While this was happening my mates were stood in shock and then Wally jumps in and pushes him back. Bri shouts "Come on then I'll fight the fucking lot of ya". While this was going on my head starts to clear and I realise what's happened. Ryao shouts "Right then, let them fight". There was a few pubs together with glass fronts and everyone was at the windows watching. As I walked towards him my legs were still like jelly and my mouth was cut and bleeding. We were in the main street that runs through the centre of town and all the cars had stopped because they couldn't get passed. At first we both miss a few punches then BANG I catch him with a big left hook and he goes down. When that punch landed I broke my hand and broke his jaw. I seen his eyes roll as he went down and his head bounced off the tarmac on the road. I drag him off the road to where it had started by the pub and got on top of him and let him have it again. When I got off him I spat blood in his face, I looked down at him and it looked like he was dying. The ambulance arrived in about a minute and got an oxygen mask straight on him and I could see the life draining out of him. At hospital he was very close to dying and was on some machine. I was worried because I really thought he would die. Luckily he pulled through. He wanted to press charges but I had too many witnesses to say he'd started it and the CPS kicked it out. Years later I bumped into him at a party and I guess everyone thought it would kick off. We both looked at each other and then smiled and shook hands. It's all water under the bridge now and we have mutual respect for each other.

One Saturday night I went to the bar to get my free drink and the owner who's a millionaire was stood there and said "Richy did you work tonight" I said no and he then said "If you never worked tonight you don't get a free drink". What a greedy man he is, someday he'll be the richest man in the cemetery. I told him to "Fuck off" and he said "You fuck off". I bit my tongue and was tempted to chin him but never. I said "Howay let's go" and about twenty lads followed me outside. There was always loads of people hanging round me, I was like the pied piper. When we got outside the owners brand new BMW was in the car park, it was about three days old and a couple of the lads started to smash it up. I got barred from every pub and club he owned even though it wasn't me.

I came out of a nightclub in Middlesbrough one night and a lad came up to me and said "I've seen you fight three times and you are fucking awesome, I'd just like to shake your hand", I shook his hand and he looked over the moon, then he went back to his girlfriend and they walked off. There was a DJ friend of mine called Mick and he told me a story about one of his friends and swears it's true. His mate was in the bedroom with the headphones on and the music was filling his eardrums, he also had his eyes shut and was having a wank. He heard his mam shout that his tea was ready so he shouted 'ok'. He finished his wank and when he opened his eyes his tea was on a tray right next to him on the bed. I don't think I could of went back downstairs, I'd of died with embarrassment.

Me and Vul were working this bar and there was a bus load of Boro lads in taking the piss full of drink. We tried to be friendly with them but they weren't interested and there was definitely gonna be trouble. The manager was beside himself with worry. We made phone calls and got a posse of lads down. We turned the music off and I went over with the lads behind me. I said "Right clever cunts it's your choice, KICK OFF OR FUCK OFF", Then I repeated myself so they all heard me "KICK OFF OR FUCK OFF". Now the odds were even they didn't fancy it so we started taking their drinks and they all got up and left.

One night on the door we got a call there was trouble upstairs. I was the first one on the scene to find one of our doormen called Frankie, On top of a lad on the dance floor keeping hold of him but also covering up as about five of the lads mates were booting fuck out of him. I dropped the first one I came to and the others arrived straight away and laid into his pals and they took a hammering. Frankie said they were booting him for about a minute and he kept sneaking a look and saying to himself 'The lads will be almost here' but the DJ never put the call out so we never knew until someone ran in and told us. I had some nasty words for the DJ at the end of the night and he filled up with tears and packed in working there. He didn't realise Frankie's health was on the line on that floor and things have a habit of taking a turn for the worst. Luckily he was ok.

There was a rave at Stockton and people from the North-East were fighting for control. There was a power struggle going on with plenty in hospital after guns, axes and knives were used on people. I worked on the door there for four weeks. It was full of paranoia and hatred and I didn't know who was who. There were a lot of dodgy characters in there and I could feel something was gonna happen and packed in. A week later the people who lost it regained control of it, I got out just at the right time. I hated raves but was persuaded to go to one this night. As we were stood in the queue two bouncers popped their heads out the door and pointed at me and closed the door. My face was well known through working at that rave so I think they thought I was linked to certain characters but I wasn't. I was in there one hour and thought I was in danger so I left with a friend. As we went out a car pulled up full of geezers. I never looked at them but I knew they were staring at me and I thought I was gonna take a bullet. We jumped in the motor and left. The car with the blokes in followed us for a few miles and then turned round and headed back. That was my finish with them paranoid places.

My friend Eddie who was Vul's cousin died in a van crash. It was a total shock, Eddie was a good un. There was an excellent turn out at the funeral and we all hit the drink for a few days.

I was in a boozer with Vul and in walked Big John (6ft 4in and 18 stone) and his pals. Vul told me about Big John taking the piss in Eddie's pub after he died. He wouldn't pay for drinks and wanted a lock in, he was trying it on. They finished their drinks so I stood in front of the door. As Big John got near me I hit him with a right hand that nearly took his head off. You'd think he was shot in the head by a sniper. He was laid flat out and an ambulance was called. As they carried him out one of his mates came back in and said to me "Do it too me, go on, fucking try it with me". I flattened him as well and he was laid next to Big John heading for the outpatients.

CHAPTER 20

I used to drink with some lads from Middlesbrough and Stockton, real good lads. I'd go through there some weekends and other times they'd come through here. There was a good crowd and I always enjoyed myself when I was with them. When they came here we'd go to a pub called The Square Ring and stay until six or seven in the morning. Everyone could relax there and we had some good nights.

I went back to work with Mick Sorby. I always got on well with Mick and I respected him, he was a good bloke. Whenever people came in a pub and we were on the door they'd think twice about starting anything. Mick had a sidekick called Peter who I'd known since I was young. He got a good baseball batting round the head one night and was never the same after it. He started to go a bit strange. He was a nice man who wouldn't normally do anyone a bad turn, after the head injuries he received, he started getting on people's nerves and was totally out of character. I started to do a few light weights just to tone up and I was weighing eighteen stone by then. Me and Mick done loads of jobs together, Debt Collecting, breaking jaws and beating people up for money, Taxing Drug Dealers. We'd go to drug dealers houses and slap them or punch them, what ever was needed, and take the drug money off them. They were only scumbags anyway so it made no difference to us or anyone else for that matter. We had some nice little earners. I also used to beat people up for money. So and so wants to know if you'll break so and so's jaw for £500 or such and such wants such and such beating up and is willing to pay a grand. Jobs like that were always coming my way. One time when I went to give a drug dealer a slap I

said to Mick "Wait here I'll only be a minute". Mick said he heard a commotion and wondered what was going on so he got out the car to have a look. When he entered he saw the dealer in a sitting position on the floor all dazed with blood streaming down his face from a cut eye and a plant pot stuck on his head with the soil dripping on to his shoulders and I was having a word with him. It was another money job. Mick pisses himself laughing when he thinks about that. I had a rule that I would never go to anybody's house when there was children present, No Way, that's where I drew the line. We met this other dealer in a car park because we pretended we wanted to do business with him. He was driving around in a nice BMW and he was supposed to be a bobby's toot. We took his car off him and told him to fuck off before he got
hurt; The BMW was a ringer so the fella couldn't go to the police. We drove around in it for a day and then thought we better get rid of it and sold it for two grand. There was another geezer who turned up in the town out of the blue, No one knew him or had ever heard of him before which was a bit suspicious. He was wanting to meet me and Mick. It's very odd when people from out of town do things like

this and you wonder what the motive is. Anyway we met him in a

pub and he started pulling bundles of money out trying to impress us saying he was this and that, He was full of shit. The dickhead even said he was an expert knife thrower, Very impressive. We took his money off him and told him to fuck off and never to get in touch with us again and to put it down to experience. We counted the bundles and it came to six grand, Lovely. There was a lad called Stevie who worked the door for Mick. He was a proper Billy Liar and we used to call him Stevie Tallstory or Bang Bang. Almost every time you seen him he'd say "I done these two blokes earlier, You should of been there, I just went Bang Bang and they were both out" or he'd say "Just after you left these blokes turned up looking for trouble so I let them have it Bang Bang and they were laid out". These fights were just his imagination
and nobody had ever seen any of them. He liked a drink and when he drank he had loose lips and liked to be loud. His ex wife was living with an old work mate of mine and I bumped into him one day and he told me that Stevie was bad mouthing me to him and his ex wife when he was full of drink trying to act like the big man. I went to his flat but he wouldn't open the door, He was pretending he wasn't in but I knew he was because I listened through the letterbox before I knocked and heard him in the front room. I shouted through the letterbox I was gonna rip his head off for bad mouthing me and I'd have him within a couple of days. I didn't know but he'd just been cashed up for a compensation claim. He went to see a mutual friend and he phoned me and said "He's very sorry for what he

said and can't remember it because he was drunk but it will never happen again" and then he said "Come to my house he's left something for you as an apology. When I arrived my mate handed me a nice wad of money and said "He's two grand for your trouble". I said "Tell him he's ok but to keep his mouth shut in future".

I used to see a half caste girl in the nightclub with a couple of lasses. Every week I'd see her on the dance floor bopping away and I'd stare over and she'd smile at me. She was gorgeous and her hair was as black as a raven's wing. I asked to take her home and we hit it off straight away and we fell in love. Her name was Linda and she had two kids, Ashleigh and Grant. I was as happy as a pig in shit. I asked her to marry me and she accepted. We wanted it very quiet with two witnesses and Mick Sorby was best man. Everyone was sworn to secrecy and there was only eight people in attendance. We didn't want a big do with loads of people it wasn't for us. We went for a drink after and I phoned people up and told them I'd been married. They were all shocked and I think they thought I was pulling their legs but I bet they all said the same thing "Why wasn't I invited".

Something happened with a couple of lads, then someone I know got involved, they involved someone else and it snowballed. I was supposed to be involved but I wasn't and was supposed to be saying this and that which I wasn't. Sorry I can't be more specific. The lies were rife. Bri Cockerill and Maori were involved and Bri bashed a couple of them. People were causing trouble so me and Bri would fight each other. People were telling him I was saying stuff about him and vice versa. There was trouble brewing. Big Irish was on home leave for stabbings and was in jail with Maori's brother and wanted to get it sorted out before someone was killed. He acted as go between and organised a meeting in a pub. We sat down and got it all sorted out. Maori told me later he had a Magnum 45 tucked in his waistband just in case. We organised a drink and went to a few bars with Irish while he was on his home leave as a goodwill gesture.

We were in this boozer with Irish and Maori and others. Irish's wife had been seeing this big ginger lad on the sly and he was stood near us with his pal and I noticed they were getting clever with Irish. I saw Maori's face and said "What's up", he said "Irish is gonna stab these two and he's got a blade under his coat". I said "Mind this drink". I went over to one and BANG he went down and out, then I turned to the big ginger one BANG he went down and also got a kick in the napper. He was in a bad way and was rushed in hospital. I didn't realise how serious he was, he nearly died and had a blood transfusion. They were gonna get carved up that's why I done it. At the time I just never thought and it nearly had disastrous consequences.

Maori took me through to meet Bri Cockerill and we shook hands. He was twenty three stone of muscle and built like a tank, he looked awesome. He seemed like a nice guy and we got on well. We've been friend ever since.

One night in a lock in with Mick, there was a banging on the door and when the boss opened up it was the armed police in their bullet proof vests wanting our names. We found out a few days later why. There was a lad over the road waiting in the shadows with a gun, he was waiting for me to come out so he could shoot me. Someone must of known what he was going to do and phoned the police. They went down and sure enough he was there with a shooter and they nabbed him. When he was in jail he got his nose bit off.

Maori's brother H got out of prison and we got on well. A lot of people didn't like him and were frightened of him but once you got to know him he was cushty. He used to come to the pub and have a few beers with me and Mick. He was a gun for hire and up for anything.

Me, Maori and another lad drove over to this estate where we arranged to meet some guys we had trouble with. We got out of the Land Rover and walk over to them. Before we can say anything they pull out guns and start to fire at us. The three of us had the same idea, run like fuck back to the Land Rover and as we're running I can hear bullets whizzing past my head. We jump in and pull away like Damon Hill and all the windows get shot out, how none of us died I don't know. People were looking out their windows with the sound of guns going off. We got away ok but our mate was shot through the shoulder. He's sat in the back clutching his shoulder, white as a ghost and looks like he's going into shock. We get to the hospital and drop him off in emergency. We must of looked a right sight pulling up with all the windows shot in. Maori and me were lucky to get away unscathed but we did walk around looking like Don King for a few weeks.

I went somewhere with a few lads to see a bloke who owed a lot of money to someone. We got there and he was alone and the lads gave him an unmerciful beating. I went out of the room as I didn't want to watch, he was getting hit with sticks. He sounded in terrible pain so I thought I'd better put him out his misery. As I went back in the room he was unrecognisable, his arm was snapped in half and the bone was sticking out through the skin and one of his eyes was completely shut. My stomach turned over when I seen it. I went over and hit him on the side of the jaw with a big right and he went out like a light, at least he was out of pain. I didn't go on another one of them. Out of the few lads who were there, one is doing life for murder and another one is dead.

There was a group of lads who got in the pub all the time and one of them was a stocky lad with a skinhead. My pal Darren told me he was an up and coming fighter and would soon be a name in the town. He'd beaten some good lads and was well respected by his generation, he was early to mid twenties. One bank holiday there was trouble in the pub, Me and Mick flew over to sort it out. One of their crowd was fighting so I grabbed hold of him to throw him out and this stocky lad grabbed my arm and said "Leave him", I said "He's going out and if you don't shut it you're going out after him", he replied "I'm not", I passed Mick the lad to put him out because my attention was fully on the stocky lad challenging my authority. I didn't speak I just hit him with a cracking right hand and he hit the deck. I thought he was trying to get up but he was in spasm and I booted him in the head and there were gasps from people, the lad was then unconscious. His mates carried him outside and an ambulance arrived and they started working on him because he'd almost swallowed his tongue. He came round and it took about thirty minutes for them to leave. The police were there and they kept telling him they knew who done it so say his name and we'll arrest him right now but he wouldn't grass. I was starting to think that if I stayed on the door, sooner or later I was going to end up in prison so I was thinking about chucking it.

One weekend when Mick was bad I worked with Peter. He loved fishing and used to skipper a boat, he told a few of his pals to come down and have a drink with him. They turned up late and the pub was empty. One of them was 6ft 3in and twenty stone and his arms, chest and shoulders looked like a pro bodybuilders but he was all natural. They were pissed and fooling around and I said jokingly to Peter "Put that big one out Peter". The big fisherman went berserk and wanted to fight me but when he put his hands up, his legs buckled and he staggered. I could of destroyed him but I don't take liberties and said I wouldn't fight him because he was drunk, I had visions of killing him. After the big fella calmed down we agreed to fight the next week when he was sober. During the week Peter came to my house with Mick Sorby and said the big fisherman didn't want to fight me and was very sorry for the way he went on. He also asked if it was ok for him to call by the pub and buy me a pint and tell me himself, I said yes if he wants to. On the Friday he came in full of apologies and said how sorry he was and bought me a pint and then left. I've never seen him since.

I'll tell this story how I was told it. I can't remember it because I was far too drunk to remember any of it. One night years ago a good few of us met in a pub at 7o'clock on a Saturday night to celebrate my birthday. Everyone was buying me drinks and getting me a double whiskey to follow. I was reluctant at first to drink the whiskey because I knew I'd be drunk in no time. Once it went down I got the taste for it and washed every pint down with a straight double whiskey. You can only say no for so long because all you get in your lug is "It's your birthday you boring bastard, Get it down ya". We were all getting into the swing of it and by 9:30 I was pissed and that's as far as my memory of that night goes. After that the taxi's came and we went to the town going from pub to pub. One of the lads who was with us was also called Richy. He had caused some trouble with some lads who were on the dance floor enjoying themselves. He decided to get stuck into them and fighting broke out, I never seen any of this or I was oblivious to it because I was so drunk. Everywhere we went, these lads seemed to be in the same place and Richy was always straight over fighting with them. Now I don't know about you but if I was out on somebody's birthday the last thing that I'd want to do is fight because it spoils the night. If I was sober I guarantee there'd of been no trouble because I would of nipped it straight in the bud. These lads were from out of town and were having a good time before he started chew with them. There was about 30 of them but they were scattered about in different pubs. As the end of the night approached I was propped up against the bar because I could hardly stand. Everyone had gone home drunk or gone elsewhere because it was too quiet where we were but I said I was staying put and there was only me and Darren left. Darren was in the club somewhere talking, when he'd had a drink he could talk a glass eye to sleep. In the meantime all these blokes from another town had met up and were enraged at the trouble this 'Richy' had been causing and headed for the club he was at. The Bare Knuckle fighter Bartley Gorman was once told "They will come for you when you are drunk Bartley", that was certainly the case with me "They will come for you when you are drunk Richy". At 1-45 a.m. a crowd of 30 geezers were outside the nightclub asking for 'Richy'. The doormen wouldn't let them in because they knew there was going to be trouble and they didn't want the place smashing up. According to the lad I was talking to at the time, we were at the bar and he could hardly understand what I was saying as my words were so slurred. A bouncer came over and said "Richy, there's about 30 blokes outside want you and they are looking for trouble". Most of them were stood there with empty Newcastle Brown Ale bottles in their hands, 30 armed men against one unarmed man who could hardly stand up because he was so drunk. The big brave bastards. I told the bouncer I was coming out and he went back down stairs. The lad said I looked at him and said "I'll have a bit of this" and he said "Don't go down there or you'll be killed". I took no notice and started down the stairs to the entrance and the angry mob. He went to the big bay window that looked out onto the street and seen all the angry people waiting for me as I made my way to the pavement arena. I didn't care, I was a gladiator. As I got out into the street I was attacked with bottles over the head, Punches, Kicks and elbows. I was fighting on memory as I fought tooth and nail and as my punches were landing they started hitting the deck. The bouncers were stood watching and the other lad was stood open mouthed watching the action from the bay window. I was taking a beating and getting attacked from behind with bottles smashing over the back of my head and I went down and got kicked unconscious. My head was jumped on and kicked about like a football. I was told I put seven of them in the outpatients but the lad watching from the bay window said he counted nine so I gave a good account of myself considering the situation. I was taken to hospital by ambulance and after being examined I was put on a ward. I remember waking up and staring at the ceiling thinking something wasn't right. As my eyes started to focus and my mind started to wake up I turned my head around and realised I was in hospital. I thought "What the fuck am I doing here". I sat up and as I did the pillow came with me because it was stuck to the back of my head with dry blood. The room was spinning as I had the mother of all hangovers and shouted for a nurse, When she came I asked her what I was doing in here? She said I was admitted with head injuries and the doctor wanted to see me this morning and that if I hadn't been so drunk, I would of died. She asked if I wanted any breakfast and I said yes. As she went to get me some I quickly put my clothes on and left. I looked like the Elephant Man (Because my head was full of lumps and cuts and not because my flies were open). I found out that day what had happened and it was quite a surprise. How come Richy caused all the trouble and then fucked off? Where did everyone go? How come I ended up fighting 30 men on my own? Everybody had their own story, That was some fucking birthday present I got. The street had CCTV cameras on it so I knew the coppers would be studying it, I also knew that the nightclub had a camera on the door which took in a part of the street so I made a phone call to get the tape. The police beat me to it and had already been and demanded it. People came to see me and wanted to put bullets in these people but I said 'No'. I said I'll fight any of them or all of them one at a time but nothing came of it. Time is a great healer and I don't bare grudges against any of them, Shit happens. They were lucky I wasn't sober because I knocked nine of them out and I could hardly stand up I was so drunk. If you live by the sword you die by the sword and that's the way it is, you've got to accept it. The police turned up and asked about the fight the night before and I said I couldn't remember any fight and they asked if I would like to press charges if they find them and I said "No chance" and told them to forget it and they left. I would rather of died outside that club than grass anyone up. I bet the filth enjoyed themselves watching that tape over tea and biscuits. I bet they wore the fucker out.

CHAPTER 21

I never learned to drive until I was twenty eight; I never wanted to drive until then. One day I just fancied learning so I booked some lessons with a friend of the family called Tony who ran his own driving school. He had a good pass rate and I had about a dozen lessons with him and he didn't charge me full price either which was cushty. When the day of my test arrived I was nervous and had an hour's lesson to calm my nerves before the real thing. I coped with it very well and stayed relaxed throughout and after we arrived back the examiner said the magical words "I'm pleased to tell you, you've passed". I was over the moon. Tony said as the examiner walked passed him after the test he said "These lads are getting bigger".

My mate Andy used to call in a flat were two lesbians lived. The butch one just looked like a man, there was nothing feminine about her at all. Her brother lived with Andy's mother that's why now and again he'd pop in and sometimes I was with him. They seemed ok and sometimes they came to the pub where I worked for a drink. They done a few drugs but that was there business, they were old enough to think for themselves. One night they came to a nightclub at Redcar with a few of us. While the butch one was dancing, I could see a lad starting to get clever with her and I knew there was gonna be trouble. I waited until it was gonna kick off and went over and the lad squared up to me in a boxers stance. I got tore straight into him and hit him with about four punches; he was laid there unable to move and covered in claret as the doormen arrived. He was fucked but his eyes were wide open because of all the crap in his system. The bouncers were pals of Bri Cockeril so it was the geezer on the deck they picked up and ejected from the club. At New Year there was a geezer in the pub selling ecstasy tablets. I found out and went over and gave him a slap and took then off him, I told him that no drugs were sold in this pub. I gave them to the lesbians so they could have themselves a happy New Year. They were getting their gear off a father and son who's E's I'd taken off the bloke and they thought the dykes had set him up but they hadn't. The next time that they got gear off the father and son they were set up and one of them took all the blame and got eighteen months in prison. In the meantime there was a bloke in the pub waving a stun gun about so I took it off him and escorted him from the premises. I put it in my coat pocket and completely forgot all about it. The next day I was on my way to Mick Sorby's and was passing the dykes flat so I called in. The door was open which was unusual so I thought I'd caught them taking their shopping in. As I went in I walked right into a drugs bust and was apprehended. I was strip searched and they found the stun gun in my pocket what I'd forgot was there. I told them how I came across it but was arrested and taken to the station. I was the very first person in Hartlepool to get done for a stun gun. They didn't know what to charge me under but it came under the firearms act, they've probably changed it now. At court I was gonna plead not guilty but my solicitor said if I did I'd get community service, I did 180 hours of that years ago and hated it so I pleaded guilty and got a fine.

I blamed the father who set the dykes up for my fine. I bumped into him one morning outside some busy shops. I hit him with a right to the body and a left in the face; he never went down but staggered and ran over the road. He was shouting that he was gonna have me shot. I left because the shops were crowded and there was too many witnesses, I was told later that he had a broken rib and broken nose. I talked to my mate H about it and he said to take the threat serious because he'd known him years and it was the first time he'd heard of him being paggered and his pride will be hurt. Maori made a few phone calls and H was right, there was a hit man coming from Newcastle to put one in me. Maori got it stopped. Another night me and Maori were stopped by the armed response police and the jeep was searched for firearms. Some lads went past a nightclub in Stockton with masks on and fired a few rounds at the doormen who dived for cover and the police thought Maori had something to do with it but he never. If I poured petrol on my arm and put a match to it, that would be the only fire arm I had anything to do with.

I saw Mick Sorby punch somebody once with a cracking shot. The lad just stood and looked at him, then he started to run and after about ten steps he collapsed and was out. It's the best delayed reaction I've ever seen.

We went out one night and there was this bloke with us, when I first started boxing in the late 70's he used to go. He was a few years older and was short, squat and powerful. He had a couple of fights in the ring and packed in, he thought he was a right hard case and jack the lad. I hadn't seen him for a number of years because he got a big stretch for an armed robbery. We were going from pub to pub and he happened to be one of us, how I don't know. The more drink he poured down his neck, the more he was getting on people's nerves shouting how hard he was. He shouted to me "Oi you outside", now I thought the prick was just joking but he wasn't. "I'm the best fourteen stone you'll come across" he screamed. Off comes my coat and we step outside. Someone shouts "Do him Richy", the pub had a glass front so everyone could see us. He came straight at me and BANG I catch him with a short powerful left hook and he folded like a ten pound note and hit the deck, what an anti-climax. I bent over him and put about four rights on his chin and he was on another planet. When the ambulance stretchered him away about fifteen minutes later with an oxygen mask on, he was still sleeping. His jaw was broke in four places so they had to put a steel plate in with screws to fix it. I had no sympathy for him because he brought it all on himself with his big loud mouth.

I went for a private sitting with a clairvoyant and got some really good messages off him but one thing that did frighten me was when he said "I can see a lot of fist fighting with you" then he got hold of my hands and said "I can't tell you to stop fighting but if you continue and you don't start pulling your punches, I can see you killing someone someday". I had already had a few lucky escapes with people at deaths door and took that as a serious warning and started to slowly take a back seat. Me and Linda were getting a divorce, she filed for it on the grounds of 'unreasonable behaviour'.

I had to have a sit down and have a think about what I was doing with my life because it looked like I was on a death wish.

Another lad on a death wish was my pal H. He got in some trouble in Lincoln and his father wouldn't stand guarantor for him. That was the last straw. He'd been tortured by his father all his life and had a stammer because of it and resented him for the misery he caused him. When he wouldn't stand guarantor it pushed him over the edge and he went to his father's house. A big argument erupted and H pulled out a gun and shot him three times, once in the head, chest and kneecap. His father was laid on the floor in a pool of blood not moving. H must have been thinking about looking at a life sentence and thought fuck it I've had enough; he put the gun to his temple and pulled the trigger. His father miraculously survived but my mate H died. It was a sad time for all concerned. The last time I seen him alive he made us both bacon and toast and we had a chin wag. I think of it like the last supper and have some fond memories of him.

I packed the door work in; I had to really as I wanted to get away from all the trouble. I still went out for a drink and it followed me, I couldn't get away from it. I walked in a pub with Mick, Freddie, Peter and Johnny; I went to the toilet while they went to the bar. There was a skinhead in there looking the worse for drink. He said "What's your name", I told him and his chest came out another foot as he put his hand out for me to shake it. Peter followed me in and was watching the proceedings. I went to shake his hand and he pulled it away and said "Dry your fucking hand first". What a cheeky cunt, I put a left hook on his chin and as he went down he smashed his head off the toilet and was laid out with blood pissing from his head. I went to the bar and said to the lads "Howay were going". They were just about to pay for their drinks so they put their money away and left as the barmaid was shouting something at them. The lad recovered but that's when I thought that I better stop going out drinking as well or like the clairvoyant said "someone will die". So I started to change my life and try to find a bit of balance and take a back seat. I wanted to leave that part of my life behind.

Me and Linda had got divorced but after a few months we got back together, I never moved back in with her it was a girlfriend-boyfriend thing and we got on great. It was a case of 'can't live with her, can't live without her'. We've been together eight years.

There was a advert on the TV quite often by Plan International showing children in the third world starving and wandering were the next meal was coming from, No education, Some as young as five would have to work all day just to put food in their bellies and walk for miles for some drinking water. We don't know how lucky we are really. Every time the advert came on I saw the pain and suffering in the children's eyes and thought I'd become a sponsor. I sponsor a girl in Ecuador, South America called Jomayra. Their life is much better these days and she is getting an education. If she becomes ill she will be seen by a doctor due to the sponsorship, most families can't afford to see a doctor when they are ill so they end up getting worse. Plan have also built a well in Jomayra's village so that everyone has access to clean drinking water. They have also supplied a health plan and vaccinations. I have been her sponsor for five years now and it's very rewarding. We exchange letters and she always tells me how grateful she is and calls me foster parent. I send her two presents a year as well as cards and photos. She was seven when I started to sponsor her and she's twelve at present and the difference in her over five years from the first photo to the present one is amazing, She hasn't half grown. It's great being a part of another family's life who live on the other side of the world. It opens your eyes as to how people in other countries live.

I was looking through the paper one day and seen a picture of a woman and she looked gutted, She'd had her African Grey Parrot stolen and it was her pet. She had kids and they were missing it to. I got a phone call from Brian Cockerill asking for my help, He said a friend of his had her parrot stolen and was there any chance I could make a few enquiries. I said I'd see what I could do, It was the same woman I'd read about in the paper. At the time I was getting an aviary built out the back because I fancied some canaries.

My mate Ste had a pet shop and was building it with the help of Mick Sorby. Ste said he had just been offered such a parrot and told me who by. The lad was a friend of Mick's and so me and Mick went to see him and I said I'd leave him alone. He had sold it on to a parrot dealer for £200 and gave us the address so we paid him a visit. We told him the parrot was stolen and we wanted it back for its owner and the money he paid for it he'll have to forget about. It wasn't on the premises so he was told to go wherever it was and bring it to my house or face the consequences. We were in the back garden doing the aviary when he turned up, When he seen the aviary he started to laugh because he thought it was getting built for the parrot and we were pulling a fast one. I told him to come with me to the woman's house so he could see for himself. When we arrived with her beloved pet she was over the moon and so were the kids and the parrot responded straight away to them. The bloke told her the story of how he came across it and she couldn't thank me enough. Brian Cockerill phoned me and said he owed me a favour and thanked me. She was in the paper a few days later and there was a picture of her reunited with her parrot but I told her to keep my name out of it and she did. I love happy endings. A couple of the lads were calling me "Richy Horsley, Pet Detective".

I got a job and went back to work installing heavy electric cables. The first job I was on was at I.C.I Wilton and I was there a few months. I.C.I was very strict on safety and at all times you had to wear hard hat, safety boots, goggles, overalls and gloves. Even on hot days when your goggles were steaming up with sweat and you couldn't see you weren't supposed to take them off. The cable always came on big round drums and once you got the drum in the place you wanted it, you put a jack either side with a steel bar running through the drum and then it would be jacked off the floor ready to pull the cable off. Sometimes it would go in a trench or up a riser but mainly it was on racks and it all had to be held in place with cleats, it sounds easy but its hard work. The big drums can weigh as much as nine tons. Once when I was working in Edinburgh we were rolling a drum that weighed about six ton and it went over my foot. My steel toe collapsed and came through the side of my boot and my toes came up like puddings. I was lucky because if it was another inch over I would of lost my toes. We were working under the canal and the tunnels went on for a couple of miles. We renewed the cable there and there was always toxic gasses being released and we used to have to make a hasty retreat back out. I worked all over the country, Barnsley, Manchester, Widness, Newcastle, Reading, London, Derby, Middlesex, Scotland, Portsmouth, Southampton, Bournemouth, Rhyl, Cardiff and plenty of other places. I once had a piss on the roof of the Hilton Hotel in Park Lane when we were putting some cable in, I was busting and the toilet was too far away. Sometimes there'd only be half a dozen cables to pull in and once you done that you were off somewhere else. One day you could be in Leeds and the next in London, I liked it better like that instead of being stuck in the same place. I had a friend in Liverpool who let me, Wally and Darren stay at his council flat. He lived with their lass but kept the flat on and the first night we had a hot bath each and because the water hadn't been used for that long, it flooded the flat below us, what a carry on. We went to a job at Derby for about six weeks and I had a look for the house we stayed at in '75 & '76. It was in Boyer Street but it had been pulled down and new houses had been built but the old pub at the end of the street was still there but I forget its name. While I was at Derby I got a phone call off Maori, it was bad news. His son Mark had just died of Leukaemia, he was four weeks past his eighteenth birthday. It was a tragedy, Mark was a lovely lad. Me, Wally and Dickie went home for the funeral and I was one of the pallbearers, it was a very sad time.

One time when we were working in Liverpool before I got the keys to my mates flat we were staying above a pub in St.Helens. One night I went out for a drink with Mark and Dickie. As we were going from pub to pub I seen a face I thought I knew and couldn't think were from and then it dawned on me, It was the famous Rugby player Andy Gregory. I went over and said "Hello Andy, You don't know me but I'm working round here and just like to say hello", He shook my hand and asked were I was from and seemed a nice fella. In another pub I heard "Not you again" and it was him and we laughed. Later in the nightclub I spotted him at the bar so I went over and tapped him on the shoulder, When he turned round I said "Are you fucking following me" and he started laughing and repeated "Not you again". He had a good sense of humour.

On the job in Liverpool there was a new mush who started for us called Trevor who thought he knew everything, On the way down there on a Monday morning he done everybody's head in. As soon as we got on the job he was running around like he was the boss and talking to people as if they were idiots, He had an overpowering personality. He was a cheeky cunt and I let him get away with a couple of remarks but when he said another thing I thought I'd teach him a lesson. He was in a cherry picker with a lad called Varley.
I shouted "Varley bring that fucking cherry picker down here now" and he did straight away. I dragged Trevor out of it by his harness and nearly took his head off with a slap and swear he done a full twist in his boots just like Michael Jackson. For a couple of days he walked around like he had a big purple birth mark down half his face. He never talked to me out of turn again. He said to one of the lads "I never want another slap off him as long as I live".

We went to London and I took a day off and spent a full day in the Tower of London, the day passed too quick for me but I really enjoyed it, I love history. After that we went to Scotland for six weeks to put the cable in on a place in the middle of the firth of forth. We had to get on a boat to take us out and we'd pass through the Forth Bride, I never realised how big that bridge was and what a fantastic sight it is. We used to have our dinner on a barge. We had some of the local lads working with us and one of them became a friend of mine, he was called Gregor and we hit it off straight away. He'd tell me a bit of Scottish history about William Wallace and the like and I enjoyed our chats. A couple of years later he emigrated to Australia but he still sends a Xmas card every year even if it does arrive in January. We stayed in Dunfermline, right opposite the abbey where Robert the Bruce is buried. I went to his grave to pay my respects. Our gaffa was a bastard and everyone called him little Hitler, he'd been on with the firm for years and was very strict. One morning I was really hung over and never had the strength to lift the cable, I'd been nightclubbing the night before in Dunfermline. I said to the gaffa I needed the van keys because I was fucked and jumped on the boat back to shore where I slept for the rest of the day. As tea time approached I got the boat back over and the gaffa looked at me in disbelief and because of my cheek he said "I'll pay you for today but don't let it happen again". Good Result. Anyone else would of been thrown to the sharks so to speak.

A few of us went to Stirling to watch the Irish band The Saw Doctors. It was one of the lad's birthdays as well and he came along and had a birthday to remember. Wherever we were in the country we always had their music playing in the van so when we found out about the concert not far from where we were working we had to go. It was packed out and everyone in the place was up dancing and singing as they played song after song, the atmosphere was great. What a brilliant night it was and what a fantastic band 'The Saw Doctors' are.

Me, Dickie and Wally went for a historic day out in Scotland. We went to Bannockburn were the Scots won their fight for independence in 1314. The battlefield is partly built on and I couldn't help wandering if anybody has woken up in the middle of the night with the screams of battle ringing in their ears. We went in the visitors centre and Robert the Bruce's helmet and chain mail were on display and bolted to the wall on the end of a small chain. He let me put it on and I had my photo took, it was bloody heavy. We took a camcorder with us so we got the day on video. From there we went to the William Wallace Monument and it was a fabulous place well worth a visit. They have Wallace's sword in a glass case. It's the actual sword that was taken off him in 1305 when he was captured by the sheriff of Dumbarton. When the monument opened in the 1800's, the sword was moved from Dumbarton castle where it had been kept since the capture of Wallace, to its new residence in the monument.

The bloke who owned the cable firm was a millionaire and once you got to know him he was a nice fella. He owned Houses, Clubs and Businesses. In one of his clubs the manager & manageress were taking him to the cleaners saying that stuff was being stolen but it was them taking it and selling it. They were a pair of cheeky loudmouthed bastards who always had to have the last word. He wanted them out but wanted to do it legally so he got papers drawn up for the manager to sign. He knew he wouldn't sign them and that there'd be trouble so he phoned me and asked for my help. After we agreed on a price he came and picked me up and we went along. I told the manager to sit down and said "Listen to me and listen good, If you open your mouth just once to speak or answer back I'm gonna break your fucking jaw, Now listen to what the man has to say and sign the papers and you'll escape with your health intact, Do you understand ?". He said 'Yes' and knew then that his game was up. His woman must of as well because she never came into the room and stayed out the way. The papers were signed with no problems and they were evicted. When I was paid I noticed a beautiful pot statue behind the bar of a Bare Knuckle Fighter and asked about it. He said the amount of people who had tried to buy it to no avail was nobody's business. I said I'd like to buy it and he gave me it as a present. It still stands tall and proud in my bedroom. The boxing promoter Frank Maloney has the exact same one in his house, I seen it one day on the TV programme 'Through the Keyhole.'

CHAPTER 22

I worked on the cable installations for three years. Sometimes we got a bit of local work where we got home at tea time but most of the time it was away. We had a bit of local work at Newcastle and we were there a couple of months. We had to pick up a new starter from Peterlee called Lee. The lads tortured him until they got to know him, he even had his coat set on fire while he was still wearing it. I was shocked to read last year in the local paper that he'd been knocked over and killed by a taxi.

I went with a few lads to watch a friend of mine fight at Sunderland. The guest of honour was the American heavyweight puncher from the 70's called Earnie Shavers who I loved watching fight. I didn't really believe he would be there but was excited at the chance of meeting him; I kept saying to the lads "He won't be here". Anyway Graham pointed and said "There he is", I couldn't believe it was him. There was a professional photographer there and he took our photo with Earnie. I shook the great mans hand and asked him who was the best fighter he ever fought and without hesitation he said "Muhammad Ali". About a week later the photos arrived in the post. I got them blew up and the lads got one each, I got mine framed and it hangs on the stairs.

Graham who was with us was coach at the Boys Welfare and asked me to come to the gym so I went a few times and just watched. While I watched I was soaking up the atmosphere and it was getting in my bones again and I started to help out with the youngsters. Once a year there was a coaching course and it was due in a few weeks and he asked me if I wanted to go on it and get qualified so I said yes. It was held in Sunderland and I went on it with Neil Fannan from our club. I hadn't done any training for god knows how long and after the first day I was wiped out. I had to go through it all again the next day and I was stiff as a board. I was sweating buckets and one of the instructors said to me "You should leave the beer alone the night before you come here". I hadn't had any, I was just unfit. The weekend after was free but the one after that was another two days of hell. Neil was my partner throughout and when we were going through various blocks and combinations I'd slip a hard one in his ribs when he wasn't expecting it and he'd give me a "You crafty cunt" look. Then just when I'd relax and forget about it 'Bang', I'd cop the same treatment and I'd look at him and he'd have a big cheesy grin on his face. The course was over two weekends and the days were long. Here's the first weekend, take a look.

PART ONE - SATURDAY

9-15. Course Assembles.
    Review of programme.
    The A.B.A. coaching scheme.
    Examination procedure.
9-30. Basic skills (practical).
10-45. Break.
11-15. Roll of the coach.
12-15. Basic skills (practical).
 1-00. Lunch.
 2-15. The sport of amateur boxing.
 3-00. The A.B.A. club.
 3-45. Break.
 4-15. Basic skills (practical).
 5-30. Equipment essential for club and boxer.
 6-15. Close.

I thought "Thank fuck for that" but there was another full day to look forward to tomorrow.

PART ONE - SUNDAY
9-15. Course assembles.
9-30. Basic skills (practical).
10-45. Break.
11-15. Coaching boxing skills.
12-00. General first aid (Theory/practical).
1-00. Lunch.
2-15. The A.B.A. rules.
3-15. Discussion.
3-45. Break.
4-15. Basic skills (practical).
5-30. Competition and the A.B.A. medical scheme.
6-15. Close.

After a weekend like that I admit I didn't fancy going back to finish it but I wasn't going through all that for nothing and wanted that badge. The two weeks came round like a week and before I knew it, we were all back there and it felt like we'd never been away.

PART TWO - SATURDAY
9-15. Course assembles.
9-30. Basic skills (practical).
10-45. Break.
11-15. Seconding.
12-15. Basic skills (practical).
1-00. Lunch.
2-15. Essentials of fitness.
3-00. Fixed load circuit training (Theory/ Practical).
3-45. Break.
4-15. Basic skills (practical).
5-30. Discussion.
6-15. Close.

I thoroughly enjoyed that, give me more. I wish Sunday would hurry up and come round.

PART TWO - SUNDAY

9-15. Course assembles.
9-15. Basic skills (practical).
10-45. Break.
11-15. Organising a gym session for junior boxers.
12-15. Running as a conditioner.
 1-00. Lunch.
 2-15. Basic skills (practical)
 3-15. Course revision.
 3-45. Break.
 4-15. Basic skills assessment.
 5-00. A.B.A. rules assessment.
 5-45. Discussion.
 6-15. Close.

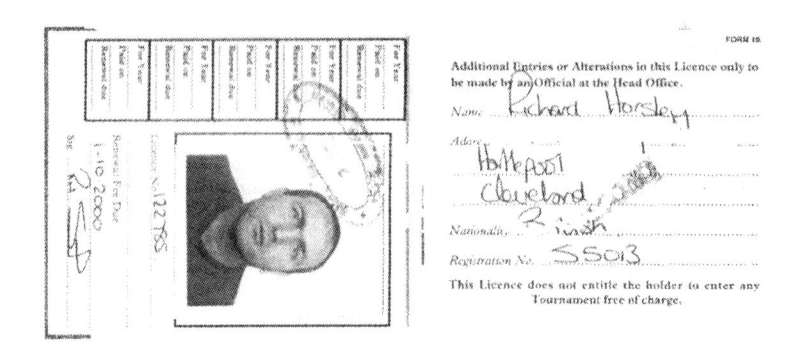

It wasn't that bad after all was it? A few weeks later me and Neil got our results and we both passed with flying colours.

It was a unique time in Hartlepool amateur boxing the '98-'99 season, especially the Boys Welfare. Everybody seemed to come together from far and wide and we had three boxers in the National A.B.A. Finals, a feat never done before in the town and never likely to be achieved again. We had some good lads, senior and junior.

We had a lad from Tunisia called Mo who said he'd boxed out there and wanted to box for us. He was raw and needed schooling but he reached the National Novice Final where he was out pointed. There was two lads fresh out of the army who came for a change of scenery to box for our club and one of them was an England international. Super-Heavyweight Billy Bessey and Lt-Welter Kevin Bennett. Billy's brother Chris won six National A.B.A. titles and regularly came up here to a boxing show or for a night out, Chris was a nice fella and down to earth. One night I was sat in a club watching England fight USA and I was sat in between two of the England boxers. Chris was captain and a Lt-Middle and the other side was Ian Cooper who boxed at Middle. Ian gave me his vest and medal from the fight because he knew I appreciated anything like that, it was a very nice gesture and I framed the vest. He was a class act and reached the national A.B.A final at Lt-Middle in '96 but went
one better the next year and won the title at Middleweight.
I became close friends with Kevin Bennett, I liked the way he was polite and had nice manners. You go a long way when you have both and he did. An old gypsy bare knuckle fighter from years ago who lived round these parts used to say "It's nice to be important, But it's

important to be nice". I like people who have manners and I hate to see bad mannered children, it's not nice at all. The first fights Benny and Billy had for our club the show was a sell out and they both won close decisions. Benny fought a Russian who was over here boxing for a Sheffield club. There was a huge following and everywhere the lads boxed there was always a good crowd of supporters. We had some good nights up in Scotland and we were always invited back. When we left clubs there would be a crowd of people in the hall all clapping us off because they appreciated the quality of boxers our club had. They couldn't believe that one club would go up and beat the best lads in Scotland. We always had a warm welcome and a couple came down to watch the lads in the A.B.A's.

I took two junior boxers to the Royal Armories at Leeds; there was another club from the town going so we shared the petrol. Graham gave us a van to go in and said the brakes were a bit iffy but just pump it and it'll stop, I didn't like the sound of that. On the way to pick the other club up I came to some traffic lights and there was no brakes, I pumped and pumped and it still kept going, lucky nothing came my way or it would of been a head on collision. I was thinking "This cunt has set me up", Graham was always doing things like that. When I got to the club to pick Timmy and his boxers up I said "Timmy you can drive that I'm not, it's a fucking death trap". There was a few hair raising moments that night and we were nearly killed a couple of times, when Timmy got out his hair was grey.

I was still doing a bit on and off with the cable installations. I was working with a lad who was Commonwealth Cruiserweight champion in the 80's; he brought the title back to Hartlepool from Australia when he knocked the champion out in the eleventh round. Stewart Lithgo was as tough as old boots and was still no mug. He fought Frank Bruno and big Frank hit him with his best shots and couldn't put Stewey down, it was stopped on cuts and Stewey protested furiously. He still runs and hits the bag a few times a week.

We had five boxers entered in the A.B.A.'s and before the first round of the regionals we all posed for a photo and it's a great line up. Three of the lads fought the reigning National champions in the

North-East finals. At Lightweight Mo Helel lost a very close decision to Andy McLean, Lt-Welter Kevin Bennett beat Nigel Wright and at Middleweight Ian Cooper lost to John Pearce. With the three we had left we realised we had a great chance of going all the way. The Semi-Finals were held at the York Hall in Bethnal Green and it promised to be a cracking show. We went to Charlie Magri's sports shop and I had a good chat with him. Charlie was World Flyweight Champ in '83 and his fights were all action affairs. We talked about various fights and fighters and we got talking about George Feeney. Charlie said that he came to Hartlepool as an amateur and boxed George and won on points. When he and his coaches left the club they were followed and chased by a gang of skinheads, he said they ran like hell with the skinheads in hot pursuit but they never got caught. He never fought in Hartlepool again after that. When I got back home I relayed that story back to George and he laughed his head off and said it was true. Most of the skins were his mates who never took too kindly to their pal getting beat. Charlie then asked me how Michael Hunter was doing and that he'd be at the semi-finals tonight and said "I'll see you there". I bought a blue pair of Everlast mini boxing gloves off him and they still hang in my car. After we left his shop, Me and my pal Wally went to a pub called the Blind Beggar and had our dinner. The pub was made famous when East End gangster Ronnie Kray killed George Cornell in there with a bullet in the head. The record playing on the juke box at the time of the murder was by the Walker Brothers called "The sun ain't gonna shine anymore" and as Ronnie was walking out he said "The sun ain't gonna shine anymore for George". It's changed a lot since then and has been refurbished and is a family pub now and they do some nice scran. We went back to the York Hall for the weigh in and everyone started to think about the job in hand. As fight time approached, the place was packed out and everyone was buzzing. First up for us was at Bantamweight, Michael Hunter boxed excellent and won a wide decision and with that he went into his third National A.B.A. final in a row. He was Flyweight champ in '97 and Flyweight runner up in '98 but trying to make the weight was killing him and he had to move up to Bantam as he was still a growing lad. Then our Lt-Welter Kevin Bennett was in action. I've never seen Benny more fired up than he was before this fight, he really did have the eye of the tiger. He tore straight into Jon Honney and ripped him apart. It was all over in 45 seconds and Honney had been down twice. During the interval I was going through the bar and I heard "Alright", I turned round and it was Charlie Magri and I couldn't believe he remembered me. He said "Michael Hunter won hey" I said "Yes" and we talked for about 30 seconds and he went back into the hall. Our last man was Super-Heavyweight Billy Bessey. He fought a big fella from Swindon and stopped him in the second round for a clean sweep. We had three in the National finals.

The biggest day ever in Hartlepool amateur boxing history arrived and a few coaches made the journey to the Barnsley Metrodome to support the lads. Ironically our three boxers were up against three lads all from the same club, Repton in London. They are the biggest amateur club in the country and have been for years. First up for us was a cracker as Michael Hunter slugged it out with Andrew Wallace in a thriller. Hunter came on strong in the last and it was anyone's title. The decision was announced as 10-9 to Hunter. Then we had Kevin Bennett against Danny Happe, as we were walking to the ring all the hair stood up on my neck with the noise and electricity, the roof nearly came off. Benny was all over Happe in the first two rounds and Happe hardly threw a punch because of the onslaught. He did connect a few times in the last round but we had Benny winning by a couple of points at the very least. The decision was announced as 9-8 to Happe and there was some booing. Benny said "I'm absolutely gutted. I won that fight, I'm sure of it. I've worked really hard all season and had no easy fights. I think I deserved a bit of luck and I didn't get it". We were all gutted for Benny, if anyone deserved a title it was him.

At Light-Middleweight we cheered for Chris Bessey, Billy's brother, if they both won tonight it would be the first time since the Gilbody's in 1980 that brothers had won A.B.A. titles on the same night. Chris beat K.Hassaine from Balham in London by a score of 17-6. It was his sixth A.B.A. title, he won one at Welterweight and five at Light-Middleweight and he's second on the all time list with only John Lyon from St.Helens winning more with eight titles.

The last fight of the night saw the last Hartlepool-London encounter. It was the big men, The Super Heavyweights and it was Billy Bessey against Joe Young. It turned out to be a thriller and the crowd went wild. The bell ended the second round and Young hit Bessey twice and Billy wobbled on unsteady legs back to the corner. All looked lost and Young should of been disqualified, I think he would of if Billy had stayed on his stool but Graham said "Go out and win it the proper way". Billy's nose was bust and there was blood all over his face and he'd taken a couple of counts. Young was looking for the winner when Billy pulled out a big one which landed flush on the chin and Young was counted out in the third to spark delirious scenes. Billy said it was the best punch he'd ever thrown, he also said "It was the best moment in my life". He wrote himself into the record books, not only as an A.B.A. champ but also as one of only a handful of brothers to do it on the same night. In the local paper Graham said "I'm so pleased for him, he has lived in his brother's shadow throughout his career and to win an ABA title is a tremendous and fitting reward for him". Underneath that it said: It was also a fitting reward for the Welfare coaching team of Reed, Neil Fannan and Richy Horsley, who guided three boxers through to the grand finals and ended the illustrious competition with two magnificent champions.

The first few fights Billy had for the Boys Welfare he wore a white vest that looked like it had just came off Harold Steptoe's back. He said "I'm gonna have to get a new vest this one is as scruffy as fuck". I had a green Nike one and gave it to him and jokingly told him if he inherits a bit of my power from it he'll be undefeated.

All joking aside, when he wore it he notched thirteen wins in a row including the ABA Title so a bit of the magic did rub off on him.

CHAPTER 23

I was staying at a pub in Battersea called The Hope. We were working at Liverpool Street in London and on dinner times we'd go and get some scran and sit on some benches and watch everyone go about their daily business at fifty miles an hour. The pace of life seems to be so fast these days. When we finished that Job we went to Cardiff and pulled the cable in on the Millennium Stadium. It all had to be done for the opening of the Rugby World Cup which was a few weeks away so we all worked our bollocks off and made the deadline. What a magnificent place the Millennium Stadium is and I'm glad I can say I worked there. When we finished the Job, a few of us got laid off because there wasn't much work in. That week one dinner time I went in the betting shop and picked some horses out in

an each way accumulator bet. At night in the digs I checked the teletext and they came in. At dinner time the next day I called in for my winnings and got £800. Me and Linda went to the Scottish Highlands for a week. We love it up there surrounded by mountains and rivers and the scenery is breathtaking. You can relax and totally chill out. We've been there a number of times but always go to different places and also go on days out to towns and villages, Fort

William, Ben Nevis, Grantown-On-Spey, Isle Of Skye, Inverness, The Trossachs and Loch Lomond are just a few of the places we've been. I recommend it to anyone. We normally feel a bit depressed when we come back because we wish we were still there. After one such holiday I went out with some of the lads. I was in a club and one of my old boxing pals Andy Tucker was working the door. He came over when I was at the bar and we were having a good natter about the old days when this geezer comes squaring up to me in a boxer's stance and starts flicking out punches. Me and Andy both knew him so I told him to pack it in. Now he should of stopped then and everything would of been hunky dory but he never. I had a quick scan of the place and a lot of people were looking and I started to feel embarrassed as he was still flicking out the Jab. I put my drink on the bar and flattened the guy. I apologised to Andy and left. Another night spoiled over a dickhead being clever. A few weeks later I bumped into his older brother who used to train amateur boxers and he said "What the hell did you do that to our kid for". I told him what happened and he was told a different story but said he knew his brother could be a nuisance when he'd had a drink. He also added that his Jaw was broke in two places and it was wired up. It's only rarely I get down the town now, there's too much hassle and it's not worth it. I've been there and done it all.

I got a phone call from Maori one afternoon and he said he wanted to see me. I met up with him and he said a few thieves who he knew had been trapped nicking some wood from a yard. As they done a runner the wood man shouted "Richy Horsley will be round to punch your heads in". They had targeted his yard on a number of occasions and were spotted a few times and got away, each time they had been threatened with me. He could of went to the bobbies but he never. I was told he'd used my name four or five times so me and Maori went to see him.

When we got there I never even knew the guy and I asked him why he'd been using my name and he said "What do they call you like", I told him and he replied "So you are Richy Horsley" then he denied ever using it. I told him I knew he had and to stop taking the piss and he admitted it but he said he'd used it only the once. I knew then that he'd used it a number of times and told him he could use my name but I wanted paying for it. I told him I knew he'd used it about five

times so I'll be back in twenty four hours to get what's owed to me and I want £500. As we were leaving Maori gave him the back of his hand. The bloke was beside himself with worry and phoned the police. There was someone at the yard buying wood when the cops were there talking to the wood man and they were on about an ambush. He made a phone call and told what he had heard and said don't go back there. The time we were supposed to be going back all the cops were laid in wait for us but we never turned up. Within the hour they had bust Maori's house and locked him up for Assault, Threats to kill and Demanding money with menaces. Maori was told he was looking at some jail for this and they'd be trying for a remand. I got a phone call from Maori's brother Robbie for me to get on my toes so I made a hasty retreat. Someone who knew the wood man very well went to see him and promised him if he dropped the charges he'd be left alone and there would be nothing else said. He needed reassuring as he was in a terrible state of fear over it. He told the lad I was getting my door kicked in at three in the morning by the police and the lad had a good talk to him and he seen the light. He phoned the cops and told them he was dropping all charges so they came out to see him and tried to persuade him not to, then they said they'd give him another twelve hours to think about it and return. When they went back he still told them he hadn't changed his mind and he wanted to drop the charges and Maori was released. The wood man was left alone as promised. What a carry on over someone using someone else's name when they shouldn't. I think a lesson was learnt for everyone involved. Kevin Bennett and Ian Cooper hung up their amateur vests and turned professional and Neil Fannan took out a trainer's license. Neil had loads of amateur fights and had about twenty as a pro at Lt-Middleweight and was given his trainers license straight away. They asked me if I'd get my license to be a second so I said yes. I had to go to a meeting of the Northern Area Boxing Board of Control and answer questions put to me by members, they asked about four or five. Dave Garside, former British Heavyweight Title Challenger spoke up for me. I then had to wait outside the room for five minutes before being called back in and I was told that my application was successful.

The local paper came out and took some photo's of Me, Neil, Benny and Cooper and done a piece on the back page about the 'New Stable'. Dave Garside got his promoters license and was putting his first show on at the Tall Trees in Yarm and the lads were making their debuts. The show was a complete sell out and a huge success.

We were relaxing in the hotel beforehand and the Eddie Murphy film The Nutty Professor was on the TV. We were in hysterics at it and were crying with laughter. Neil hadn't seen it before and was laughing that much he was slavering all over the place. It certainly got rid of any nervous tension and both Benny and Cooper won their fights impressively. They led the way for the new crop of fighters in the town and will soon be challenging for British honours. Garside put some really good Sunday afternoon shows on which were always sell outs. Michael Hunter also turned pro and is unbeaten; he'll soon be winning titles. I was house second for about five shows and worked all our lads' corners. At one Sunday show there was a table about six feet behind me with the two guests of honour sat there. One was Earnie Shavers who I mentioned earlier, he fought twice for the World Heavyweight Title losing to Muhammad Ali and Larry Holmes. The other was former British Champ Brian London who also fought twice for the same title losing to Floyd Patterson and Muhammad Ali respectively. Brian was originally a Hartlepool lad but moved to Blackpool when he was young. His father Jack London was from Hartlepool and was British Heavyweight Champion in the 40's. There used to be loads of open air boxing shows in the town in those days outside The Engineers Club. I've always loved Hartlepool and hope I never have to move, the town has some great history. The town itself used to be known as 'Little Chicago' because of the amount of gangs it once had. There was the Captain Cutlass gang, The Turquoise gang and loads more. Lots of tough foreign merchant seamen came to this town because it was a thriving sea port, they would spend their cash in a row of pubs called 'The Barbary Coast'. I remember a story that a prostitute opened up Captain Cutlass' face with a broken bottle leaving him scarred for life with a big mars bar down his face. A man I would have loved to have known was 'Battling' Manners; he was the town's first bouncer. He was a hard as nails Man Mountain who didn't suffer fools gladly and would literally bounce them out of pubs. He worked here in the 30's, 40's and 50's and once fought as a pro Heavyweight boxer. All the old timers said he was a real character and a fighting machine.

Buffalo Bill and his Wild West show came to the town in 1904.
People from Hartlepool are called 'Monkey Hangers', the name dates back to the Napoleonic wars. A French galleon was shipwrecked off the coast of Hartlepool and the sole survivor was a small monkey that clung to some wreckage that drifted ashore. The monkey was dressed in a miniature French uniform and the local crofters were illiterate and thought the babbling monkey was a French spy. They must have got confused with the word 'Powder Monkeys' whose Job it was to supply the gunpowder to the French gunners. The crofters conducted a speedy trial on the beach and found the poor monkey guilty of being a French spy. The monkey was sentenced to death and the poor bastard was hung. So there you have it, I like everyone else in Hartlepool am a 'Monkey Hanger'.
A guy from Wales called Julian Davies got in touch with me and came up with a couple of his friends and done an interview with me for a book he was doing called Street fighters. Over the past year we've had many conversations on the phone and I regard him as a good friend. I'm on the front cover and also the first story in the book.
There was a story about me in the local paper talking about some of the brutal street fights I've been in and about the forthcoming book. A member of the local boxing board said if I wanted to carry on working in the corner at boxing shows, I'd have to go in front of the board and answer questions about the Street fighting. I didn't want to sit in front of a bunch of people while they put me on trial, anyway I didn't see what business of theirs it was so I packed the corner work in.
One morning last July I saw our Debbie's fella walking up the path and thought "I wonder what he wants?". When I opened the door he said "Jackie's dead", it took the wind right out of my sails and he said Debbie was in a hell of a state. I asked what happened and he replied "She killed herself". I couldn't get my head round that, Jacqueline wouldn't kill herself, she had six children at home and they were her life, she doted on them. I said I was going straight round to see Debra but he said she was visiting family and wouldn't be back until two

o'clock. I was in a daze when I went to see Debbie, she was in the kitchen making a cup of tea and her eyes were red and bloodshot with crying. I was also choked up with red eyes. She said Jackie had phoned her a few hours before she died. Jackie said that her oldest son Andrew who was nineteen and who she hadn't seen for years had turned up out of the blue a couple of weeks before. He was eating her out of house and home and wasn't giving her a penny. She said to Debra that he was a stranger and was thinking about asking him to leave but was worried what people would think. She had been married to Paul and then got divorced but they were still together, although he wasn't living with her. Deb told me that Paul had punched Jackie a couple of years ago and knocked one of her teeth out, I didn't know any of this or I would of put him in hospital. Jackie had six kids at home, the oldest two were Stacey and Damien who were from a previous relationship and the four youngest were Paul's. Jackie told Deb that her and Paul hadn't been getting on and he was being very difficult. That afternoon she went to a pub to see him and he was all over a woman who's name I'll leave out. An argument erupted and she stormed off. When she phoned Debra at 9-45p.m. she told her what had been going on and after a few minutes said "I'll have to go because I'm going out".
Debbie:"This late".
Jackie:"I'll phone you tomorrow".
Debbie:"I'll be at work".
Jackie:"I'll phone you after work and tell you what's happened".
Those were the very last words they ever spoke and what happened after that we don't know. Paul has changed his story about five times and I know he's hiding something.

Paul and Andrew are the only ones who know what really happened and Andrew was having nightmares for weeks after. But what really did happen they have on their conscience for the rest of their lives. Paul said Jackie went upstairs and they could hear her walking about, she sat on the bedroom floor and had a cigarette. Then she wrapped the lead from the hoover around her neck tightly about nine times and passed out through lack of oxygen to the brain. When he went upstairs he struggled to get the door open as she was laid against it but as he went in he seen the lead round her neck. He said her eyes were vacant and he knew she was gone. The ambulance came and found a faint pulse and gave her the electric shock treatment but couldn't bring her back. That was at 1-30a.m. At 2-00a.m. she was pronounced dead. She was only 38. Paul said there wasn't a suicide note. If Jackie was thinking about killing herself she would of definitely left a suicide note. The six children were asleep in the other bedrooms. The post mortem said the cause of death was strangulation by ligature and at the inquest there was an open verdict. I went with Debbie to the hospital morgue to identify Jackie and the marks on her neck were visible. We were shocked to see our sister like that. Me and Deb done some running around sorting the funeral out and the undertakers done a good Job, they were very helpful. The day before the funeral I had one hour alone with her and was talking to her and crying my eyes out. She looked beautiful, just like sleeping beauty. The morning of the funeral I had another hour alone with her, I wanted to say goodbye to my sister in private, it was very personal to me. There is a turquoise stone that is sacred to the American Indian and I put one in her sleeve and kissed her. The funeral was very emotional and I still haven't got over her death. There's not a day goes by that I don't think of her. She smiles at me everyday from a picture I have of her on my wall. I have a little soft spot for her daughter Stacey as I looked after her for a short time when she was a baby so there's a little bond there with me. Paul is looking after all the children with the help of his family but I think he's robbed them of their mother so I don't bother with them.

Two months after Jackie passed away, my mam's second husband Ken died. He'd been in a home for a few years and died of natural causes. I was at three funerals in five months last year.

My Mam's friend Annie Bobbin, her adopted daughter Joanne died of kidney failure just before Christmas and was buried on Christmas Eve. She left an eight year old daughter, who is now getting brought up by her Grandparents. There was another friend of mine who died before Christmas and she was the same age as Joanne, both only 25 but she choked on her vomit. You can be talking to someone one minute and they'll be gone the next. Life is so short; you have to make the most of it while you can because we are not here very long.

I heard of a good medium that lived in a town not far from me so I had a private sitting with him and what he told me was unreal, he was spot on with everything and everyone. I got messages from me Dad, Granny Horsley, Sister Jackie and my pal H. He said Gran was with her sister Margaret, I didn't know who she was so I asked my mother if Gran had a sister called Margaret and she said yes but she died when I was only a child. He also said "Don't take this the wrong way but I feel you've got away with murder", "You are very lucky you are not doing a long time in prison", "I can see a lot of fighting with you and you don't know how close you came to killing someone".

I saw a medium years ago who told me the same thing. I've decided never to fight again. If those messages aren't warnings for me to stop I don't know what are. Only six months ago a lad was killed in our town with one punch. You don't only ruin your life but you ruin your families, the victim and the victim's family. It's not worth it.

I went to a Bird Of Prey centre with Tommy and George and we were having a good look round and talking to the blokes who run the place and they were always willing to give advice or answer questions. There was a flying display on and the birds would swoop down and fly just above your head and put the shits up you. The bloke gave me the glove to put on and part of a baby chick as food to put in my fingers of the gloved hand. He gave a signal and this big Buzzard came flying out the trees and swooped down onto my fist and took the chick, the power of those birds is unreal. We were there about three hours and had a great time. What was significant about it was as soon as I got home I put the TV on and all the stations were Live to America because the world trade centre was on fire after a plane had crashed into one of the towers. Then I watched as the second plane went into the other tower, I couldn't believe what I was seeing and the rest is history. I'll never forget what I was doing on September 11.

When my aviary was built I filled it with all sorts of birds, Canaries, Cutthroats, Silver Bills, Strawberry Finches etc and they bred like wild fire. I never sold any of the young; I gave them away and bred for pleasure not profit. I done that for over two years and enjoyed it but then I decided to have a break and gave the birds to my friend who has a pet shop. I cleaned the aviary out and it was stood empty for about six months and one day Tommy said "you know what would look well in that aviary", "what" I said, "An Owl" he replied. I'd never given a thought to owning an Owl before but he planted the seed and it seemed like a good idea. I bought a book and a video on Owls before I got one so I could understand them a bit more before I got one. I had a look in the local Ad Mag and there was a young eight months old Barn Owl male for sale. I phoned up and it hadn't been sold so I put my name on it and had a ride through for it with Tommy. It was at a place called Seaton Dellevell which was about fifty miles away. I had been there about twelve years before to see a Scottish Medium called Mary Duffy give an evening of Clairvoyance to a packed hall. When we arrived at the house the guy looked like a new age traveller. Out the back he had aviaries with Birds Of Prey in and knew what he was talking about and he handled the birds like he knew what he was doing. He showed us the Owl and he was a beauty. He was feeding him on baby chicks and he gave me some to take home. I also used to give him mice once a week as well for a change. I would watch him at night to see his actions because my aviary was open and surrounded by trees and birds and it was like being in the wild for him. There was a place in the end of the aviary for him to sleep and shelter. I started a new trend because Tommy bought a pair of European Eagle Owls, George who I call Bald Eagle bought a pair of Turk Owls, Mick Burns bought a pair of African Spotted Eagle Owls and Maori bought a pair of Snowy Owls. I called my Owl Barney because he was a Barn Owl and I had him for a year. When the mating season started he was calling all night for a mate and I couldn't get to sleep for him so I decided that he had to go but I wanted a good home for him. Mick Burns had introduced me to a friend of his called Gerry about eighteen months before and I often called by his flat for a cuppa and a talk. He was a great bloke and a proper naturalist and a little eccentric. When he heard I was getting rid of Barney he said he would like him so I gave him the bird and he's had him since. He keeps him in a lovely aviary and he's well looked after. Gerry was originally from a little pit village called Station Town in County Durham and was an expert in hunting with lurcher dogs and terriers and an authority on wildlife in general. When he was a younger man he was known by the nickname 'Screw' Lawson for his regular run ins with the police and he chinned a few of them in his time. He is 64 now and still active with his dogs but is a lot more sedate these days and spends a lot of time making fancy walking sticks and staffs for his friends.

He moved to the Shires and lived in an isolated cottage on his own for twelve years hunting and studying wildlife while working in the kitchens at the Military College in Wiltshire. This time his only run ins were with the Rupert's (officers) and not the police. He returned to the North-East a couple of years ago and settled in Hartlepool. He has many friends and is a wealth of information on wildlife and wild growing plants and flowers.

Mick Burns who introduced me to Gerry used to be a judge at dog shows and judged all over the place even Denmark and Holland. He mainly judged the Bull breeds and he is a good friend of mine and has been for years.
I developed a hernia just above my belly button, It's called an umbilical hernia. It's were the intestine pushes through the stomach wall, I don't know how I got it but it kept getting bigger and it looked like a golf ball. I was referred to the hospital and as soon as the doctor seen it he said "You need surgery". I wanted to lose a little bit of weight before I went in and lost a stone. You can't do any exercise when you have a hernia in case it strangulates and then you are in

serious trouble. I went in hospital on the Sunday, had the operation on the Monday and was released on the Tuesday Tea time. They cut me open, pushed the intestine back in and put a mesh gauze there so it can't push back through and then stitched me up. I've had to take it easy until it heals up and I'm going to start doing some exercise a few times a week. A bit of swimming, walking and pad work, that'll do me and I'll soon be down to eighteen stone. I currently weigh nineteen stone.

EPILOGUE

When I think of it I've been very lucky and only been down for three months when I was young. I know I've done a lot of damage to people in the past and I put it down to the way I hit. I'm a trained boxer and know how to throw a punch and would always aim for a few inches behind the target area so my fist would go through with the punch. I've had around one hundred street-fights with only one loss when I was drunk. I knocked practically everybody out but never caused any of it, there's always been a good reason for it. My hands have been broke on numerous occasions. I try to enjoy life a bit more these days so I've moved away from all the trouble and take a back seat now. I'm going down a different path now than the one I was on. A few people said to me why don't I write my life story but I wasn't fussed at first but when I had my operation I couldn't do anything and had to have complete rest so I started putting pen to paper. I've had tears in my eyes and a few lumps in my throat recalling some stories which stir up the old memories. My mother helped me with the stories when I was very young because I was too young to remember.

This book is the fourth book that I'm in. I'm also in: VIV GRAHAM 3, THE FINAL CHAPTER by Steve Richards, STREETFIGHTERS by Julian Davies and WHAT MAKES TOUGH GUYS TOUGH (6th Edition) by Jamie O'Keefe. The TV have expressed an interest in doing a documentary on the Street fighters book. There is a film being made soon about Newcastle hard man Viv Graham who was gunned down and killed and the man behind the picture has promised me a part as a film extra. Things are looking promising but I'll just take each day one at a time and see how things go.

My sister Debbie has two sons who are amateur boxers and both are canny fighters. My family consists of: Jill Louise who is coming up 20 and does a bit of singing and dancing around the social clubs. She made me a Granddad last November when she gave birth to a beautiful baby girl called Tyler Jo.

Then there's Donna who is nearly 17 and just leaving school, she is going into hairdressing. Our Terry is 15 and a lovely natured lad, he's not a fighter. He'll be leaving school next year. He goes to drama classes and does a bit of singing and dancing. They've just done two nights at the Town Hall Theatre and it was packed out both nights and they received standing ovations. Then there's Ashleigh who is almost 12 and about to go into the senior school. She is very athletic and won the County Primary Schools Championship at running three years in a row, 2001 and 02. She is a brilliant Gymnast and has loads of Gold's and Silvers in various competitions. She has just been accepted at the school of excellence. Her ambition is to be British Champion and to one day represent her country at the Olympic Games. Last but not least is Grant who is 8 and a typical boy. He is right into Karate and is doing very well going through his grades. Hopefully he will be a Black Belt when he goes into the senior school. None of them live with me but I'm a part of their lives and hope I always will be.

Well that's my story. I hope you've enjoyed reading it as much as I've enjoyed writing it.

BEST WISHES
RICHY HORSLEY
MAY 2002.

TRIBUTE FROM CHARLES BRONSON

Some men are just born to fight, it's in their blood. They can't do nothing about it, they have to fight. A fighter isn't necessary a psycho or a thug, far from it. Most fighters are gentlemen, men of pride, men of honour. Put a baby in their arms and they cry with joy like any man. But if you fuck with a fighter you've got to expect the consequences. You're gonna get hurt, you may even die. No man is invincible. Even the fighters at times feel defeat, some even die. But bet your arse on it if they don't die, they're coming back for more. Richy Horsley is one of these special breed of men and I'm honoured to know the man.

Max Respect,

Charles Bronson.

PREVENT YOURSELF FROM BECOMING A VICTIM
'Dogs don't know Kung Fu'
A guide to Female Self Protection
By Jamie O'Keefe £14 including post & packing
Never before has Female Self Protection used this innovative approach to pose questions like. Why do Rapist's Rape? Why are Women abused? Why do Stalkers Stalk? This book takes a look at all Simple, Serious, and Life threatening aspects of Self Protection that concern us daily, along with **PREVENTION** of Child abuse and Child Abduction, Emotional cruelty, Telephone abuse, Road rage, Muggers, Date rape, Weapon attacks, Female abduction, Sexual Assault & Rape, Self defence law, and what it will allow us to do to protect ourselves, plus much more. With over 46,500 words, 77 pictures and 200 printed pages 'Dog's Don't Know Kung fu' is a no nonsense approach to women's self defence. It covers many realistic scenarios involving Children's abduction as well as typical attacks on women. Besides quoting actual events, the book explains how to avoid trouble and how you should react if you get into a situation.
<u>*This book is a 'must read' for all women and parents.*</u>
It is also important for teenage women, but, due to some of its graphic depiction's of certain incidences, parents should read it first and decide if it's suitable for their child.

Foreword

Dogs don't know kung fu

I'm not usually known for writing forewords to books on self protection, and not because I'm afraid of competition, on the contrary, the more people offering good advice in the fight for better protection be better:- rather its because most of what I read on the subject is crap.

I would never be happy putting my name to something that does not represent my own views, and that's putting it mildly. Not only are the proffered 'self defence' techniques in these manuals unlikely, they are also, very often, dangerous and opinionated.

I have written some 20 books to date on self protection and related subjects so you'd think that there would be very little left for me to learn. I rarely if ever find a manuscript that inspires me or even one that offers something new, a fresh perspective, an innovative approach.

Jamie's book did all the latter. He offered inspiration and sensible (and in retrospect, obvious) solutions to the many enigmatic 'grey areas' that had long perplexed me, a so called expert.

Questions that I have been pondering upon for years were answered at the first reading of this text. So I not only commend Mr O'Keefe on writing probably the best self protection book for women on the market but I also thank him for filling in the gaps in what is, at best, a very intangible subject.

What makes this book even more unique is that Jamie is a veteran instructor with thousands of hours of women's self protection under his belt, he is also an empiricist in that he has put his training to work in real life situations. Now while this may not say a lot to the lay man/woman, to those in the know, it speaks volumes.

Most of the instructors out there teaching self protection have never been in a real situation and so garnish unreal scenarios with unworkable, hypothetical technique.

You will get no such balderdash from this cutting edge instructor. What is offered on the menu in this text will prepare you, of that I have no doubt.

Self protection in the very violent 20th century must now, out of necessity be viewed as an environmental seat belt, it can no longer be down graded as a recreational pastime that comes third down the list of priorities after basket weaving, people are being attacked and killed, every day of the week, in un-provoked, un-solicited and bloody attacks.

My advice to you the reader is to take on board what Jamie has to offer as preventive measures and make them part of your life. Being aware will help you to avoid the majority of attack scenarios, for those that fall outside the periphery of avoidance, the simple, yet effective physical techniques on offer in this book will, if employed with conviction, help to neutralise even the most ardent of attackers.

This is a great book that makes great sense.

The best of its kind.

Geoff Thompson. Coventry

BOUNCERS - SECURITY DOOR SUPERVISORS
THIS IS THE BOOK THAT TELLS IT ALL

No matter what position you hold in your workplace.
The actions of **Security** will affect your safety and that of the general public.

Do you really know all you should about Door Supervisors?

Find out how much Door supervisors should know - but don't know!
If you want professionalism from your Door Supervisors, you must read this book

If you want to become a Door Supervisor
You should read this book!
If you are a Door Supervisor, Security, or Bouncer,
You must have this book!
No matter how long you have worked the doors – you will learn something from this book

---

Order your copy now at **£14 inc p&p**
By cheque/Postal order
Payable to NEW BREED
at New Breed Publishing, Po box 511, Dagenham, Essex RM9 5DN

Peter Consterdine
Author of 'The Modern Bodyguard' said
'This book is a blueprint for the future'

Foreword
Old School – New School

Whether you want to call them Bouncers, Doormen or Door Supervisors, they are still the people with the most thankless job I know.

Constantly under pressure from their own employers, local authorities, the police and especially the general public, it is no wonder that on occasions their self control is taxed to its ultimate. At times, even the best can lose that fine sense of perspective that allows them, night after night to take the constant barrage of banal and often alcohol influenced verbals whilst still keeping the smile in place.

I'd like to think that even going back some 23 years when I first started working on the doors that I subscribed to the "**new school**" approach so creativity described in Jamie's latest book. At that time I weighed eleven and a half stone at six foot one and despite having been on the Gt. Britain and England Karate Teams for some years I knew my traditional marital arts had limited value in the very particular conditions one finds in a night-club.

My weapons were politeness, humour, intellect and large doses of patience and, at times, even larger doses of pre-emptive strikes when occasion demanded. I'm the first to admit, however, that the conditions which applied in the seventies are different to today.

I saw the change begin in the eighties when, as a club owner, it was apparent that the nature of violence, the carrying of weapons, even handguns and the influence of drugs, was going to exact a heavy toll and so it has.

Twenty years ago when someone threatened to come back and shoot me, I slept easy knowing that the next day he wouldn't even remember where he had been the night before - now you'd be reaching for the ballistic vest.

Gang warfare, drugs, control of doors, protection rackets are all now part of the club scene and in the middle is today's doormen. Some are corrupt, some are vicious, some are plain thick, but the majority are honest, well intentioned and keen to do a good job in the face at mounting pressure from many quarters and increased violence and all this with "officialdom" now peering over their shoulder.

Often lied to by the police as to their correct rights of self defence under the law. This book should re-educate people about not only the law, but the many other complex issues.

Expected to be amateur psychologists and perfect man managers versed in a whole range of conflict resolution skills, doormen are still on the 'front line', both male and female.

Door licensing schemes are supposedly the answer to the problems inherent in the profession, but they only go part way to solving many of the issues which still give cause for concern.

Old School, New School clearly defines the gulf between the two approaches as to how the work should be carried out and it should be obligatory reading not only for all door people, but also the police and anyone who has an interest in the leisure industry. By doing so they will get a very clear and honest idea about the difficulties of this work.

Old School, New School isn't just a book about doorwork. It is an effective manual on modern methods of conflict resolution. Over the past few years there has been a substantial rise in the number of companies specialising in delivering courses on conflict resolution in the workplace.

If you read this book you will have all the answers to the management of conflict and aggression.

Doormen have been doing this for years, the only difference being the fact that they have developed their skills from intuition and experience of interpersonal skills in often very violent and aggressive environments.

Now we know that this is a science just as any other form of social interaction and '**Old School, New School**' sets out to educate on the complexities of what is required.

The book recognises, however, that learning these very specialised skills will still not be any guarantee that you can create a person who can be capable of operating in this increasingly dangerous environment. The job is harder now than it ever was and don't let anyone tell you otherwise. Doing this job puts you under a microscope and an official one at that. 'Big Brother' most certainly watches over your shoulder and, many would submit, quite rightly so.

I know many doormen who should have no part to play in the industry and many people to whom the recent changes will be hard to adjust to. What I know for a certainty is that the inherent dangers of the work increase every year.

For those doormen and the people who control them to resist the pressure from others to become another drugs distribution outlet takes courage and confidence from everyone in the organisation. Many crumble and give in to the pressure and violence, but equally many don't and I hope that **Old School, New School** will give people not involved in this work, a clear insight for once, the dangers and complexity of the work. For those people who are in the thick of it, I believe that this book is a "blueprint" for the future.

Peter Consterdine

7th Dan Chief Instructor – British Combat Association

Author of : The Modern Bodyguard, Fit to Fight, Streetwise

What makes tough guys tough?
The Secret Domain

Written by Jamie O'Keefe

Jamie O'Keefe has interviewed key figures from boxing, martial arts, self-protection, bodyguards, doorwork, military, streetfighting and so on. Asking questions that others were too polite to ask but secretly wanted to know the answers.

Interviews include prize-fighter **Roy Shaw**, also **Peter Consterdine, Geoff Thompson,** and **Dave Turton** from the countries leading self-protection organisations 'The British Combat Association' and the 'Self Defence Federation.' Along with Boxing heroes **Dave 'Boy' Green** and East London's former Commonwealth Champion '**Mo Hussein.**' **Plus unsung heroes from the world of Bouncers, Foreign Legion, Streetfighters (Richy Horsley), and more.**

This book also exposes the Secret Domain, which answers the question 'What makes tough guys tough.'

Find out what some of the toughest guys on the planet have to say about 'What makes tough guys tough' and how they would turn you into a tough guy.

Available from NEW BREED at £14 inc p&p

FOREWORD
DAVID TURTON 7th DAN - Self Defence Federation

When I was asked by Jamie to write a foreword to this, his latest book, I was both pleased & honoured, and a little intimidated by the prospect.

The first seemingly obvious thing I did, was to read it..

Sounds obvious, but I mean **REALLY** read. On doing so, I found myself being drawn quite deeply into Jamie's thoughts and ideals.

Jamie tends to venture into fields that few, if any, other authors have entered. In doing so, he lays open many often-unanswered questions. He makes those of you-who have asked themselves these soul searching questions, feel that they are not alone. Having known Jamie for more years than both of us care to remember, I have the advantage of being able to 'hear' his voice, whilst reading his words. I can hear the inflections that show his passion in his beliefs, and the sheer sense of honesty of his words. Read this book with no other distractions, and give it the respect of doing so with your full attention. Only then the effort will be rewarded with the insight you will get.

I first met Jamie O'Keefe around twenty years ago. I was a Guest Instructor on an All-Styles self-defence course, and Jamie was a participant on the course, a very noticeable one at that. I thought here was a talented Karate-Ka, a bit brash, but Oh, so very eager to learn. He was mainly into what we thought of as 'Free-style' Karate back then, but searching for something more. His thirst for learning was nearly insatiable. His Black Belt status was of no real consequence to him. He simply wanted to get stuck in and learn.

He's still doing just that. ... **THE SAME ENTHUSIASM IS PARAMOUNT IN HIS WRITINGS.**

I have looked for a way to go past the usual platitudes, and try to give; what I feel is an honest appraisal of what I feel Jamie is trying to give.... Then it registered ... That's the word ... **HONEST**.. That's the man and his writings.

Jamie always 'tells it like it is'. No holds barred, and no respecter of the many fragile Egos so prevalent in the Martial Arts these days. In this, he ranks along my two other favourite HONEST Combat Authors ... Geoff Thompson and Peter Consterdine. Don't read this book for 'ways to do it', Don't read this book and be offended by his honesty. Read it, because NOT to read it, will leave a massive hole in your understandings of the World of Man & Violence.

Make it part of your collection, but keep going back to it to read it again and again.

I RECOMMEND THIS BOOK,
I DON'T RECOMMEND MANY... **'READ IT'**

At last a book just for the smaller person

Ever wondered how the little guys
Manage to beat the big guys?
Wonder no more!

I THOUGHT
You'd be
BIGGER !

A SMALL PERSONS
guide to
FIGHTING BACK
by Kevin O'Hagan

Available now at
£14 inclusive of Post and packing
Please make Cheques and postal orders payable to
New Breed
and post to
Po Box 511, Dagenham, Essex RM9 5DN

How would you like to be able to
Stop an attack in its tracks?

How would you also like to be able to do it
within a second or two?

How would you like to do it without even
having to draw a breath?

Finally, would you like to know what the
alternative to grappling is?

Then get

'Pre-emptive strikes for winning fights'
'The alternative to grappling'

by
Jamie O'Keefe

The book raved about by 'James Whale'
On his Radio Show
'Talk Sport 1089MW'

Pre-emptive strikes for winning fights
'The alternative to grappling'

by
Jamie O'Keefe
£14 inc P&P
from
New Breed
Po Box 511
Dagenham, Essex RM9 5DN

Foreword
Pre-Emptive Strikes

On first meeting Jamie O'Keefe, I was struck by his warmth and humour. I was then struck by his fists, head, & knees... Having been on the receiving end (though thankfully only in training) I can attest to the extreme effectiveness of the techniques he teaches. However, as I got to know him better, I was even more impressed by his integrity, honesty and commitment to teaching. Like many of the finest instructors and toughest fighters, Jamie is a gentleman.

These days I consider Jamie a good friend, but that's not why I agreed to write this forward. I believe he writes some of the best material available on modern self-protection, material, which can be, quite literally, life-saving.

I am proud to be able to associate my name with such valuable work

So what is the value in devoting a whole book to the pre-emptive strike?

Be in no doubt that this is one of the most important concepts for personal protection you will ever learn. Over the years I have read about, trained with and worked the door with many individuals who have vast experience of real violence. Every single one of them *without exception* recommends and uses the pre-emptive strike as the prime tactic for self-protection when a physical assault seems inevitable.

This book thoroughly dissects the theory, training and practical application of the pre-emptive strategy. From legal and moral ramifications to pre-attack indicators, from action triggers to Jamie's unique 'Strike Storage & Retrieval System', this book is the most exhaustive, insightful and thought-provoking treatise on the subject I have yet seen.

The lessons contained within these pages were learned the hard way, with spilt, blood & broken bones - this book was written so you don't have to take that route.

Read, absorb, and live by Jamie's advice. You'll be stronger and safer for it.

When talk fails and escape is impossible or impractical, the pre-emptive strike is your best option. I'll let Jamie tell you why.

Simon James
Instructor, Close Quarter Combat Systems

THUGS MUGS AND VIOLENCE

Want to know what its like when it really kicks off?

Forget the movies - this is the REAL world.

Jamie O'Keefe

www.newbreedbooks.co.uk

Thugs, mugs and violence
The story so far

In this true account of his journey, Jamie O'Keefe unveils the reality of living in the East End of London. From childhood to adult this compelling, harrowing and often highly amusing story tells of his encounters with streetfighting, crime, drugs, violence and the martial arts. It goes through the trials and tribulations of boyhood right through to his days of working on the door in the heart of London's nightlife. Read how each of his confrontations and experiences have played a major part in making him the well respected authority in the fighting arts that he is today.

This book is sure to intrigue and fascinate you so much it will be hard to put it down..

The names and places have been changed in order to protect the guilty

THUGS, MUGS and VIOLENCE

REVIEWED AS
'BOOK OF THE MONTH'
Front magazine

£14 inc p&p
from
NEW BREED
Po box 511, Dagenham Essex RM9 5DN

The Late Reg Kray telephoned me from prison, after having just undergone eye surgery to talk through the foreword for the re-print of this book.

Due to time restraints and the restrictions that he is bound by, I asked him if he could sum up his thoughts, on this book in a lone paragraph, rather than a lengthy foreword. Although Reg has given me his consent to quote him in length on all the good things that he has said about this book. I have decided to just go with the lone paragraph which was written by Reg himself. *'Thugs mugs and violence'* now has a permanent place within the cell of Reg Kray and is also read by the other inmates.

Thank you Reg for you phone-calls, sometimes three a day, to share your thoughts, ideas, opinions and philosophies with me.

Your friend
Jamie

"Jamie's book 'Thugs, Mugs and Violence' is an insight into the violent times of today and should be read"
Reg Kray – Kray Twins

Photograph kindly supplied to me for inclusion by Reg Kray

REG KRAY – 32 YEARS SERVED

1968 – 2000 HM Prison.

**A NEW BOOK
AVAILABLE NOW**

GRAPPLING WITH REALITY

SURVIVAL ON THE GROUND

KEVIN O'HAGAN

£14 from
NEW BREED

NO ONE FEARS WHEN ANGRY
by Jamie O'Keefe

£14 inclusive of P&P
NEW BREED PUBLISHING

WWW.NEWBREEDBOOKS.CO.UK

The new book by Alan Charlton

Awareness Fears And Consequences

An insight to understanding what you can do to stay safe. You may have only one chance and only one choice

By Alan Charlton

By Alan Charlton

NEW BREED PUBLISHING £14 inc P&P
PO BOX 511, DAGENHAM, ESSEX RM9 5DN
WWW.NEWBREEDBOOKS.CO.UK

In Your Face
'CLOSE QUARTER FIGHTING'
by
Kevin O'Hagan

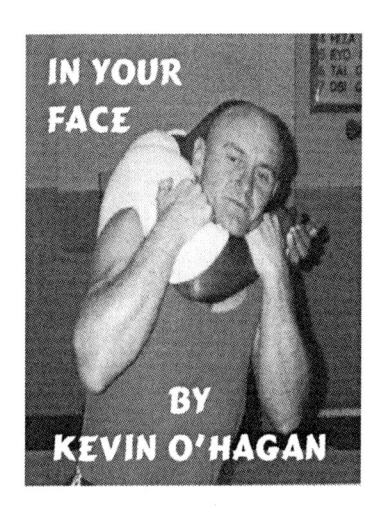

£14
inclusive of post & packing
from
NEW BREED

WWW.NEWBREEDBOOKS.CO.UK

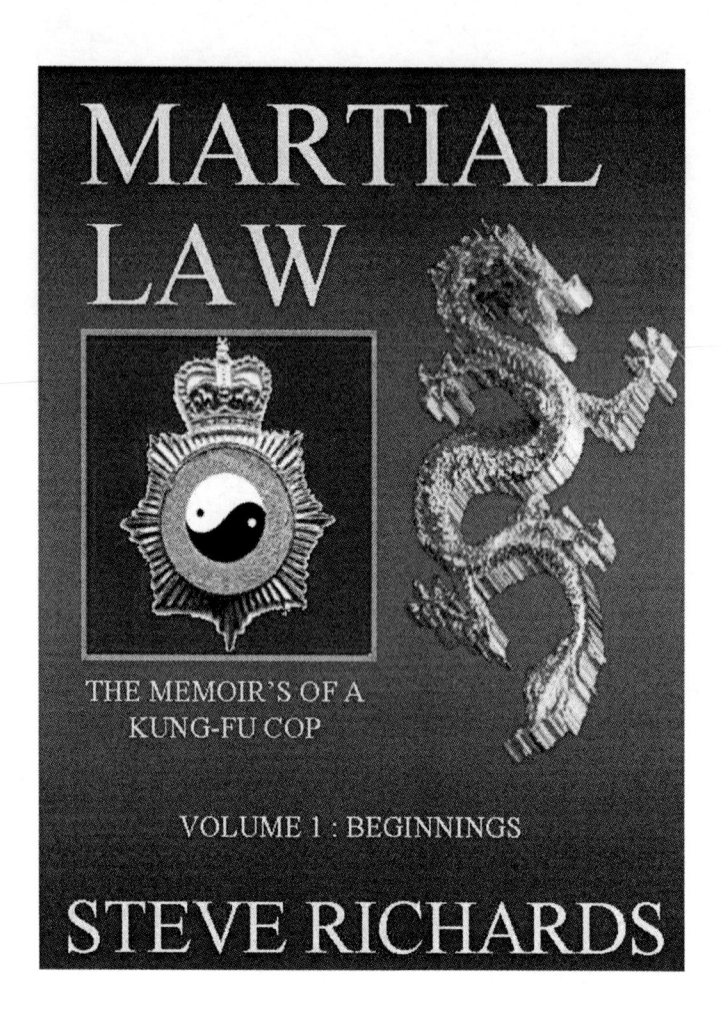

Martial Law Vol One – Beginnings – Memoirs of a Kung Fu Cop
Martial Law Vol Two – Toxteth –Memoirs of a Kung Fu Cop

This story is split over two books available at
£14 each inc P&P from New Breed

The Pugilist Quest
By D'Lambert Mensah

The thinking persons guide to Combat

£14 inc P&P from New Breed

WWW.NEWBREEDBOOKS.CO.UK

FROM BULLIED TO BLACK BELT

WHAT DO YOU DO WHEN LIFE SEEMS TO HAVE BULLIED YOU INTO SUBMISSION AND YOU ARE SO AFRAID YOU DON'T WANT TO LEAVE YOUR OWN HOUSE? YOU CAN EITHER GIVE IN OR FIGHT BACK. I LEARNT, THAT WHEN IT MATTERED, WHEN IT REALLY, REALLY MATTERED, I HAD WHAT IT TAKES TO DIG DEEP.....

A TRUE STORY BY SIMON MORRELL

Bullied to Black Belt
By Simon Morrell
WWW.NEWBREEDBOOKS.CO.UK
£14 inc P&P from New Breed

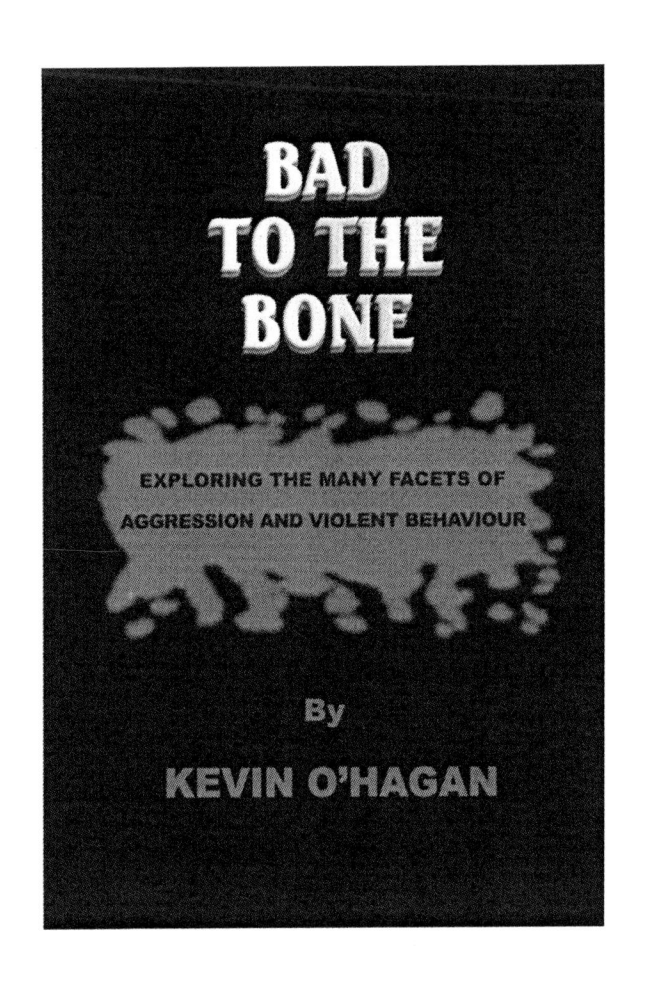

WWW.NEWBREEDBOOKS.CO.UK

Bad to the Bone
By Kevin O'Hagan
£14 inc P&P from New Breed

Trust Me – I'm a Doorman
By Kev Fisher
£14 inc P&P from New Breed

WWW.NEWBREEDBOOKS.CO.UK

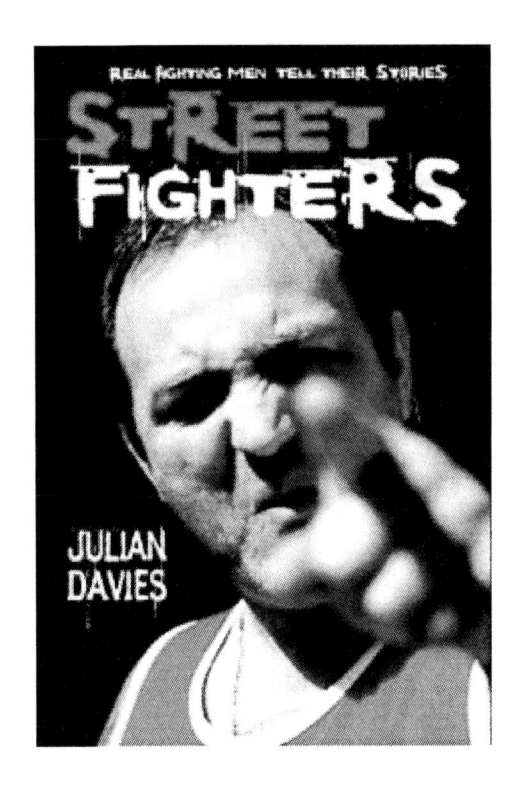

STREETFIGHTERS
By Julian Davies

This book is not available from New Breed but you can order it from major bookshops.
Features 22 real streetfighters including
Jamie O'Keefe and Richy Horsley

NEW BREED PUBLISHING
PO BOX 511, DAGENHAM, ESSEX RM9 5DN

ISBN

09517567 10 Dogs don't know kung fu – J.O'Keefe
09517567 29 What makes tough guys tough – J.O'Keefe
09517567 37 Pre-emptive strikes for winning fights – J.O'Keefe
09517567 45 In your face – K.O'Hagan
09517567 53 Grappling with reality – K.O'Hagan
09517567 61 Old School New School – J.O'Keefe
09517567 7x I thought you'd be bigger – K.O'Hagan
09517567 88 Thugs Mugs and Violence – J.O'Keefe
09517567 96 No One Fears when Angry – J.O'Keefe

09538555 11 The Glory Boys – J.O'Keefe (Still to be published)
09538555 2X Kicking it – P.Francia
09538555 38 Awareness Fears and Consequences – A. Charlton
09538555 46 Bad to the Bone – K.O'Hagan
09538555 54 Martial Law Vol One Beginnings – Steve Richards
09538555 62 Martial Law Vol Two Toxteth – Steve Richards
09538555 70 Bullied to Black Belt – Simon Morrell
09538555 89 Trust Me I'm a doorman – Kev Fisher
09538555 97 On the Chin – Richy Horsley

1-904432-00-X The Pugilist Quest by D'Lambert Mensah

Here are details of some of our books that you may want to add to your collection.

SAFETY FIRST (UK)
Training Available

Our current list of training programmes and services:
Accredited Conflict Management & Personal Safety Training
Open College Network Accreditations

- *Introduction to Personal Safety - Level 1* *
- *Personal Safety - Self Protection - Level 2* *
- *Staff Personal Safety Awareness - Level 2* *
- *Conflict Management Instructor's Training - Level 3* *

Edexcel Foundation/BTEC Qualification

- *Conflict Management Instruction - BTEC Advanced Award* *

Additional 1 & 2 Days Short Courses
- *Recognition and Resolution of Conflict at Work*
- *Staff Personal Safety Awareness Training*
- *Personal Safety/Self Defence Training*
- *Stress Management & Relaxation*

Specialist Training & Services
- *Personal Security*
- *Control & Restraint Training*
- *Close Quarter Defence Techniques Training*

Available as Distance Learning Programmes
For further information regarding our training programmes or services, please contact:

Safety First (UK), 2 Lansdowne Row, Berkeley Square, Mayfair, London, W1J 6HL.

E-mail: personalsafetyfirst@hotmail.com

Telephone: 0207 306 3399

© Safety First (UK)

www.newbreedbooks.co.uk

Newbreed
JAMIE O'KEEFE

All books are £14 each inc post & packing

1. **Dogs don't know kung fu** - A Female guide to self protection - ***Jamie O'Keefe***
2. **Old School New School** - The only training guide to doorwork - ***Jamie O'Keefe***
3. **What makes tough guys tough** - Secret domain revealed (exclusive interview with Roy Shaw) - ***Jamie O'Keefe***
4. **Pre-emptive strikes for winning fights** - The alternative to grappling fighting- ***Jamie O'Keefe***
5. **Thugs, Mugs and Violence** - The story so far - (Jamie's Autobiography) - ***Jamie O'Keefe***
6. **No One Fears When Angry** - If Anger & confrontation has affected you - read this book - ***Jamie O'Keefe***
7. **I thought you'd be bigger** - A small persons guide to fighting back - ***Kevin O'Hagan***
8. **In your face** - Close Quarter Fighting - ***Kevin O'Hagan***
9. **Grappling with reality** - Survival on the ground - ***Kevin O'Hagan***
10. **Bad to the Bone** - Exploring the many facets of aggression and violent behaviour - ***Kevin O'Hagan***
11. **Awareness Fears & Consequences** - Insight to understanding what you can do to stay safe - ***Alan Charlton***
12. **Martial Law 1** - The Memoirs of a Kung Fu Cop- Beginnings - ***Steve Richards***
13. **Martial Law 2** - The Memoirs of a Kung Fu Cop - Toxteth - ***Steve Richards***
14. **From Bullied to Black Belt** - A Journey through Fear, Agoraphobia and back - ***Simon Morrell***

To order any of the books shown simply make a cheque/postal order payable to **NEW BREED** and write on the back your full name, address with post code along with books you require. If you would like any books signed by Jamie or a message, please include that as well.

All books will be sent out the day your payment is received so *NO WAITING!*

Send orders to:- NEW BREED, Po Box 511, Dagenham Essex RM9 5DN

ALL NEW BREED BOOKS ARE PRO-MARTIAL ARTS AND WILL COMPLIMENT YOUR CURRENT CHOSEN ART